SKATING OUT OF THE VAULT

A TRANS WOMAN'S ESCAPE FROM THE GAME OF MASCULINITY

BRIANNE BRINKER

Tehom Center Publishing is a 501(c)3 nonprofit publishing feminist and queer authors, with a commitment to elevate BIPOC writers. Its face and voice is Rev. Dr. Angela Yarber.

Paperback ISBN: 978-1-966655-38-1

Ebook ISBN: 978-1-966655-39-8

CONTENTS

To: Valerie Hill

The first person to help me see myself.
You deserved to own this world, my dear.

1
CRAWLING UNDER THE BED AND INTO THE VAULT

THE ROOM WAS A PERFECT SQUARE, INCLUDING A CLOSET with sliding doors, two small windows situated over two twin beds protruding from the wall to the right of the door, with my baby brother Darren's crib nestled in between the beds. I could not miss the large window at the wall on the opposite side of the room as the door, against the wall where my bed was, the kind of window separated into four quadrants with a vertical and a horizontal divider cutting leading out to our backyard, and a big tree that grew at the back fence. I figured back then that I must have been the favorite child since I was the oldest, but also since I had the best window to see the whole backyard, our back porch, our drive-way, and the neighbor's gigantic bird feeder. It was my special place. The place where I could be myself.

I would walk past the bed near the closet and past the crib in the middle to my bed. I would grab my doll–a stuffed little boy with brown overalls, a plaid shirt, and the plastic face of a little white cherub with very little hair scratched into his head. He was aptly named 'Little Boy' and our entire house made sure they knew that it was a boy doll. A boy. Not a girl. Never a girl. He was there ever since I could remember.

I would take Little Boy and place him under the bed, and after I draped my Peanuts themed blanket on the other side of the room over the side of my bed so it covered the open area underneath, I would crawl under the blanket and inside my "secret hideout." Under here, I could not be seen by anyone, real or imagined. Unless of course, I wanted to see those who I imagined. And I did.

With Little Boy as the lookout, I would rearrange whatever was under the bed: a used, rolled up sock that I peeled off in the night and flung against the wall and under the bed in the process, a used pair of underwear, a pajama top that slipped out from under the pillow and down the head of the bed along the wall, one shoe I had not been able to find since my mom was busy with my one year old and three year old brothers, a couple of matchbox cars that were pushed under the bed during some sort of car races with my brothers, a wiffle ball, all of which was haphazardly strewn around this boy-cave among the dust bunnies. The bed's footprint was huge; seven feet by three and a half feet was an enormous cave to little ol' me with my skinny five year old body, and with the roof of the cave being only fourteen inches off of the ground, causing my bare knees to rub along the hardwood floor as I slid myself, sometimes causing my knees to turn pink or red from the irritation, and my shirt and shorts that I was wearing to be a bit dusty. I was careful to hold back my sneezes that threatened to occur from being that close to the dust. Staying low was necessary to avoid getting snagged or scratched by the wire grid that the box spring and the mattress was resting on that served as the ultimate cover. Plus sliding around close to the ground seemed more sneaky and secretive. It was dark except for the light that was allowed in from the side of the bed near the wall that was underneath the window. But moving all around the cave on my belly was necessary to be sure I was protecting my hideout cave and no one could find me. No one could find out what I was doing there.

Closing the door was not allowed due to my parents' rules, but it helped me to hear if anyone was coming to this part of the house, and if they were, if they were going into the bathroom, which was at the middle of the hallway, into my parents room, which was at the opposite end of the hallway. With our one floor living space, I could hear practically everything that was going on: the TV in the background, my mom talking to one of my brothers or my dad.

I would sneak under the bed when I could so I could be by myself. I would have a secret space to hide a spare cookie that I managed to take off of the table, the taste of it lingered in my mouth. While under there my thoughts would somehow instinctively pivot to a way to make myself feel good while I had pictures in my mind of women. Women on TV, a cartoon girl, neighbor women, or even girls my age or a little older. Or myself. The real me. We were pretty, meaning for me at the time, very styled long hair that curled at the ends and a large, warm ear to ear smile. They all would somehow know my name in those days and it seemed like I was the best friend to every one of them while secluded in my hideout cave. By this point Little Boy was relieved of his duties as lookout and became my pillow. I started to realize that this was a reason that I just had to be there, that it was not just playing pretend espionage anymore. Even though I could not describe this feeling, had never heard of this and was very confused, I knew it had to be a part of my own little secret world that only I could enter and participate in, and only Little Boy and myself would know about.

I became aware of this world when I was around five years old. In the living room, sitting, laying, or rolling around on our large, oval, braided area rug in three or four shades of brown and beige. We used to watch the old black and white TV that was located in the middle of a long console that contained a radio on one end and a record player on the other with the largest telescopic antennas, which were popular in the late 1960s and early 1970s. Often in the afternoons, we watched what was on one of the four stations available in St. Louis (five if you have an additional antenna attached which offered cartoons, Sesame Street, and older shows like The Munsters, Leave it to Beaver, Superman, and others from the black and white era). A vivid memory had me visualizing a scene where Superman rescues Lois Lane from the outside ledge on the 64th floor or something very dangerous like that. And just as the bad guy cuts the rope or whatever was holding her in, Superman shows up, saves Lois just before the rope was about to break due the gradual fray, brings her down to safety, and then flies back to destroy the bad guy in front of the onlookers, including Lois, and bring him to justice and make Metropolis safe once again. That amounted to an action show at that point in my life, around 1969-72, at age five through seven. The show implied that Lois, and every other woman, was crazy about Superman. They were not so crazy about his alter-ego Clark Kent, the mild-mannered reporter who was such a nice guy and seemed hopelessly crazy about the beautiful and talented Lois.

This made it loud and clear that the women were more attracted to the strong, tough guys and not so interested in the plain, ordinary mild-mannered guys, even though they were actually the same person portraying two different personas. But Superman is where my confusion began: I was not confused about if I saw myself as Clark Kent or Superman. I was not even confused about whether or not I would want to be with Lois Lane. My question was: Did I see myself as the hero, the strong and unbeatable Superman? Or did I see myself as the prettiest girl on the show, Lois Lane? I could not in my head come up with a definite answer to that question, and it was a question that may take me a lifetime to figure out. What I did know was that I cannot let anyone know about this question that kept racking my brain, for several reasons. From that point on, I knew this question and other thoughts related to that must never be discussed or revealed to anyone in any way. I did not know the terminology at that young age, and being the oldest child I had no older siblings and no cousins that I was close enough with to educate me about anything regarding this confusion. I just knew I could not tell a single soul. No One. Long before I had any idea about a closet for people who thought like I was thinking and felt as I felt, I knew the place I had to put these thoughts and what evolved into my true self was not a closet. I had to put them in a place that only Superman was able to bust into or out of: a secure bank vault with a door that is a foot thick, heavy with levers and dials all over the outside of it, without any of the combinations nor any keys.

This vault, which at the time I envisioned inside my head, was somehow my own alternative world. As a child around that time, I had an imaginary ladybug friend that I used to talk to, and she lived in the enormous tree at the end of our back yard. I remember years later when I actually saw a ladybug, that I didn't even know what an actual ladybug looked like at that point in time. I have come to find out that it is common for kids to have their imaginary friends that are alive to them, such as a doll like Little Boy or a stuffed animal, or some other friend. I shared conversations with my mom about Ladybug, and it was cute and fun for her. But this other thing, well, I had no idea how to explain it, and I knew I was a little boy since that is what I have been told all my life up to that point. To let them in on this secret gave me a very strong feeling even at age five that it would not go over well. For this reason I would retreat under the bed and into my private cave hideout, and I had comfort that no one could see me physically, so I could live dressed like a girl or woman in the comfort of my own head where the vault was, where no one has to know anything. At least part of me, and perhaps the most authentic part of me, along with questions concerning this Superman scenario, lived in the vault for decades.

2

DON'T CALL ME A WOMAN

I WENT TO A CATHOLIC SCHOOL, SEVEN HOLY FOUNDERS, in Affton, Missouri from grades one through eight. I was a decent student, somewhat smart. I did not study much, except for things that were easy to study for such as spelling tests and math tables and equations. Anyone in my friends group, which consisted of the other boys on our soccer and baseball teams, who would get grades that would be too good would be put down by being called a "studier" by the other kids in my friends group. We knew we were not as smart as the girls, for no other reason than it did not appear to us that we were expected to be. Yes, there were some boys that got excellent grades, but they were not totally invested in our friends group. Overall, I achieved B and A caliber work, by focusing on the essentials and not much beyond what was required. This continued until, well, the end of my Master's degree studies. My habits were formed early and I was comfortable with getting A's and B's throughout. My two younger brothers would get grades a bit lower, which would make my grades look that much better to my parents in relation.

The other putdown that we all tried to avoid was to be called a "Woman." Our friends group, along with other guys in the class, would use that word as a putdown, which in an indirect way indicated the superiority of men over women. We did not want to be considered soft or weak at that time, an appearance of anything other than tough you could be considered a woman. It was clearly a way to put others in their place for not being tough enough. I did not want to be considered a woman to those guys, for a lot of reasons, but the most important reason being, what if I am one but could never live like one? Or, what if I kinda, sorta, think that I just might want to be one but cannot subject myself to the torment that would come my way from everyone I knew? One other reason is I loved sports, and I lived to play what was considered the toughest positions, other than in soccer where I played out on the wing, I was a catcher in baseball, and a goalie in ice hockey. Up until high school, I participated in all three sports, pouring my heart and soul into my training. I put in extra workouts and prioritized my commitments over social outings, always pushing myself harder than anyone else on the field. My goal was to prove that I could be the best, and I embraced every opportunity to improve and excel.

In the third grade and older, to be called a woman, well, that just would not have worked out. In those days, the 70's, the girls and the boys were not even allowed to play the same sports, and heaven forbid they play together. Our soccer team for the school was full of very good athletes, and with good coaching. I was not as good at soccer, in fact I am not sure I even headed a ball for the entire eight years that I played. But I was fast, and could win races against defenders, which made me at least a valuable player on a very good team, one that lost maybe a total of 10-12 games in 7 years and many league, tournament, county, and city championships. We did have very good athletes; in fact, I understand that five of us from that team went on to play college sports, some of them in soccer. Perhaps one of the best athletes in our grade was not allowed to play with us. The only reason was she was not of the same gender. The boys did not even interact with the girls in Physical Education class. To this day I am not aware if anyone even thought of asking her to play, since there was no girls soccer program in the early 1970s at our school and girls just did not play soccer. She definitely would have been one of our better players and would have taken the starting spot from one of the boys (maybe mine?). She was also among the smartest kids in the class. So a girl who happened to be at the top of the class as an athlete was not allowed to play with boys? Did any of us or our parents ask why? If we wanted the best team, shouldn't we have encouraged her to play, and challenge the system to allow her to play? Nah, we left well enough alone, along with our parents, who as far as we knew, liked it just the way it was. We had it too good for us the way it was.

All of this reinforced to me that I would never be able to discuss my presence inside the vault. One thing was clear to me during this time watching these athletic scenarios like this play out from the vault was that girls were not supposed to be better than boys, and if they were, it would be arranged so it cannot be proved otherwise.

Now, for those boys who were really weak, and acted like or spent too much time with the girls, you would be considered "queer." I did not really understand what the word queer actually meant, but I knew I needed to avoid that label at all costs, risking being outed before I even knew what I would be outed for. Something inside me told me that I should be the queer one, but I did not know why until I was closer to sixth or seventh grade. But something a lot stronger and louder told me that I should not–repeat, should not ever–do anything to be considered to be queer. (The words gay and lesbian were not yet heard of at our school, or at least not used, in third to sixth grade in the 70's). Make no mistake, the use of the word queer was as a slur.

All of that was what was going on at school in grades three

through six. At home, behaviors such as paying attention to girls or acting the least bit feminine was not going to work out with my family dynamic: my construction worker father, and my stay at home mother. But I knew I did not need that when I was doing everything I could to play sports, both organized and outside in the neighborhood. All the while, the dream of playing college hockey, or even pro hockey, was ever present, a lot like so many other kids my age. In grade five in art class, I remember the question posed that we would have to draw a picture and describe how I wanted to be known. In my dreams, I wanted to be on the cover of Sports Illustrated. But I was terribly confused about these dreams; I did not know if I was on it for being the goalie for the St. Louis Blues (my hometown and favorite pro hockey team to this day) holding the Stanley Cup, or if I was on the cover as the model on the swimsuit edition. In my dreams this was a difficult decision, almost impossible. But in the real world where I had to actually live and actual living, breathing people would see this assignment, my decision came down to which Blues hockey jersey I was wearing on the cover, the road blue jersey or the white home jersey. The swimsuit edition remained in a very prominent place inside the vault.

Socially, the neighborhood kids played a lot of sports. There were a couple of kids older than me, and the rest were generally around my age or a bit younger, but not by much. We played a lot of sports. Football in the fall, and in the snow, baseball in the summer, or at least versions of baseball. And for most of the winter, it was street hockey. We would play in our two-car garage with a super slick floor with only a couple of players. We would also play on a street one block away, which was a dead end and relatively smooth blacktop. The other main place was in the driveway of one of the guys, super slick blacktop, long and narrow. With all of these, whether it was hockey on the street or stick ball on the street, we drew lines, bases, and whatever else our imaginations decided we needed. We were out there each day, after school, or whenever possible. My middle brother, Grant, played a bit, but not much. My younger brother Darren was very athletic and tough, and played outside with me often. When I was by myself, I was either shooting pucks in the garage, throwing a tennis ball against a wall to play catch with myself, or even shooting baskets at our net-less hoop attached to the outside of our garage.

While my family was central in my life through grade school, I was obsessed with the St. Louis professional sports teams from an early age. My favorite hockey players on the St. Louis Blues were Garry Unger, Barclay Plager, and Mike Liut; Lou Brock and Keith Hernandez from the St. Louis Cardinals baseball team; and Terry Metcalf from the St. Louis Cardinals football team. I could not get enough of sports, both organized, outside at home, or watching the odd game that came on television in those days, the days before every single game was televised. I read the sports section every day, and knew the current standings of all of the local teams at all times. Sports, and hockey in particular, was a lifelong obsession, and this felt like I was a normal guy doing normal guy things.

My youngest brother Darren, four years younger, had a friend his age that lived a few doors up the street. His friend had a sister, two years older than me. Our parents were friends, particularly our mothers, so us kids would be together at times when our mothers got together. She was, I could only describe then and now, very cute, and a huge, huge Blues fan. I developed a crush on her around fourth through sixth grade, maybe longer. She would hang out with the neighborhood group at times, not so much to play the games we were playing. Once in a while, I would go up to her house to hang out with her, as friends. She was nice to me and we were friends, even though she was two years older and in the middle school years, and was very attractive as she was definitely starting to outgrow a younger boy who was a sports nut. But the times we did hang out, I gathered intelligence on girlhood, observing and analyzing every interaction like a covert agent on a mission. She had long, polished nails at the time, and talked about them, and she took great care of them. I could ask her questions about her hair or whatever, and she did not seem to judge. Of course I never let on that I had a crush on her, and the part that I kind of wanted to join her when she painted her nails so she could also do mine remained in my head. The piece of it that I wanted to be her was tucked away very securely in the vault. It added to my confusion. Why would I want to dress like her and grow long hair and nails like her while I really liked her and hang out doing things that did not involve playing sports? This was beyond confusing to be sure. I was sure I liked her, but was nowhere near mature enough for her as a fourth grader and she being a sixth grader looking forward to junior high school. I was also certain that I wanted to be her sister, her twin, her best friend that was a girl and do girl things. But I also wanted to be a boy and play sports. Sports, and living as a dude the way I was being socialized to do won out, since I had a genuine love for playing and wanting to be the best I could be and do it for the rest of my life. It was also clearly the path of least resistance with the other path clearly unreachable at that point in time.

The other major reason was because, well, it was just plain wrong, or so I thought back then. Nothing in my world had signified that it was ok for a normal boy to want to dress, look like, and be one of the girls. I knew this from every single time my father referred to a guy as a "sissy," from every time that a classmate referred to a guy as a "woman" or a "queer" and from my family talking negatively about someone they thought was sleeping with someone of the same sex. I knew I had no one to confide in, and trusted absolutely no one but myself. I felt I was the only one who really knew me, and that was even suspect since I really didn't understand myself. The isolation of talking to myself reinforced the feeling that I was trapped in this vault and the conversations I had with myself that would never be heard by another living human being. Knowing these feelings at that time of my life made me feel as if I would never be able to leave this vault.

I started to realize that I really needed to think about the answer to the question, "What the hell was going on inside this vault?" It made me curious to dig deeper, and I knew it was going to be a solo operation.

3

EAT, SLEEP, SPORTS, REPEAT

I was always into sports once I entered first grade. I do not remember being all that good at any of the organized sports I played during that year, which were soccer and baseball. In soccer, I really did not understand the sport at first, and according to my mother, the head coach would always yell at me for something. I do not remember being yelled at, but I remember our assistant coach, Mr. Klein, being very energetic, a good teacher, and he was very positive. I learned how to play the game, and understood what to do on the field, even if I did not love the sport, did not want anything to do with heading the ball, and my skills were suspect at best. My mom always would tell me that she was surprised that I stuck with the sport after that year being yelled at so much, but I remembered the positive vibes, and since I do not remember it, I did not view the yelling as a personal attack. I made friends with some of my teammates, and I enjoyed it enough to come back the following seven years.

My father coached me in my first two years of baseball, and he put me in as a catcher. I did not feel as though I could catch all that well, but I did like watching the Cardinals baseball games on TV, so I figured it out. He played me at catcher for my entire first year. It was coach-pitch, so all I would do was catch the ball on every pitch when the hitter did not hit the ball, which was almost every single pitch, and throw it back. I did get a ton of practice catching balls, and the better I got, the more I liked it. It got to a point that all I wanted to do was catch things. Dad's coaching style was to be loud, and raise his voice to be heard, but he was a good teacher and nice to everyone. He could be intimidating, and around the house, we were scared to piss him off. We knew he acted tough, as if he was on his construction job as a bricklayer at times. He was great to us, and a good mentor for us boys to grow up into men-tough, hardworking men. He grew up in a large family on a farm in a small house, with no generational wealth and worked on the farm from the time he was little kid. As an adult he worked hard at his job and took on extra work on the weekends for our family to have the extra things that his regular paycheck did not quite provide, and he made sure we were taken care of as much as possible.

I started hockey the next year, in third grade, and was in love with it. I had just started skating a year prior, and I got on an ice hockey team in second grade. My coach, Don Dlugos, was the epitome of positivity, the perfect coach for young beginners and he made it so much fun to play. I think I scored a couple of goals that season, and I could not wait to get back to the rink as soon as practice or the game was over. I improved by the end of the season and learned a lot about the game; I just could not get enough out of it.

At the end of the season, there was a spring league that Mr. Dlugos encouraged team members to participate in. He asked if anyone would like to play goalie, since the goalies on our current team was moving up to the next age level. I raised my hand, and he was so excited and said the association can lend us the equipment since it is so much gear and it is expensive to try out. He was very encouraging. I loved that position. I played goalie in an iceless hockey league our school put together, and I would often be stuck playing in goal in street hockey without being given a choice. I was good at it, and I wanted to catch every puck I saw. I played that spring season, and did the best I could with the little goalie coaching I had. I watched the St. Louis Blues hockey games, and really focused on the goalies and tried to imitate them. I practiced in my room, and outside playing street hockey. My athletic ability was starting to show, and I had quickness. During this year, with the other sports I played, things got easier, and I felt plugged in. I really fell in love with baseball, and I really only wanted to play soccer for the team aspect, and I really liked our assistant soccer coach for his constant teaching and positivity.

But my first love was ice hockey from the minute I began to play, and specifically playing goalie in ice hockey. I dearly loved playing hockey, every chance I got. I begged my parents to go to the week-long goalie school when it came to our area every year, and while it was hard, it was what I wanted to do. I remember vividly the amount of time I spent looking forward to every practice and game. I would envision myself making saves, routine saves, spectacular saves, desperation saves, even thinking about some of the saves I made in the previous game, along with some of the goals I gave up to figure out what I could have done better. I loved the feeling of stopping the shooter from scoring on a breakaway, or stopping nearly every penalty shot. I really wanted to be the best goalie on the ice at practice, and made it a goal to outwork every other goalie on the ice. I looked forward to practices and games throughout the day for as long as I played competitive hockey through college. The sport of hockey and the position of goalie consumed me from the minute I started skating.

To this day I am still involved in athletics as a profession, with a career in coaching and athletic administration, because of the massive amounts of positivity and fun I had experienced and the love both of these coaches instilled in me in the entire youth sports experience. This included practices, training and development, winning and losing, team camaraderie, and so many others. The love for sport and the cause of it dominating my life for the next several decades runs through these two important men in my beginning years. I think of this every time I coach beginners in hockey (or baseball and soccer with the kids when they were younger).

I bring this up while talking about my family because my family was a big part of my being involved in sports, and fostered my love for them. My dad was sports-minded, and one important example of his sports indoctrination was way back to my seventh birthday. St. Louis Blues hockey tickets were difficult to get in 1972, and my parents had season tickets that they split three ways with two other families. When we were old enough to appreciate it, my dad would take us to a game on our birthday each year. My mom would usually go with my dad, and it was a night out for them, but we were able to go on our birthdays. In those days, everyone dressed up to go to games, and I wore my suit and my black shiny dress shoes. It was such a treat to go to those games. We would go early so my dad could go to the bowling alley across the street from the old St. Louis Arena so he could drink beer cheaper than inside the Arena during the games. During my first-ever game he took me to against the Philadelphia Flyers, I fell in love with the sport on the spot. This was before I had begun to play, but after this experience, I just had to play. I had a March birthday, which was towards the end of the season, and the Blues would clinch a playoff spot with a win that night. The building was packed, with organ music playing catchy and chanting type music during stoppages of play, and the atmosphere was the most exciting that I had ever seen before. The "LET'S GO BLOOOZ" chants by the fans echoed throughout the building, and throughout my memory until this day. The Blues won, the crowd was excited and loud, and I was amazed that after the game there was a huge pile of players jumping on the goalie, who was apparently to a little kid who was seeing his first professional hockey game, the most important player on the team. I will never forget my seventh birthday and that game, the game that was pivotal to my growing up process and would determine the trajectory of my life for decades.

With my dad, things often revolved around beer. He would go to work each day, lay brick in the cold, or the heat, or whatever the elements would bring, and it was hard. Each night, if he did not have to coach a practice of mine or one of my brothers, he would stop at a bar at the top of our street, about three blocks away. The place smelled like grill grease, and we always knew where he had been once he got home. He had smoked for most of his life to that point, and smoked until I was finished with college. He worked very hard and was good at what he did, even working for himself on the weekends for extra money to help put the three of us through hockey programs. It was what we knew. We just assumed that dads went to work then stopped off at a bar after work for beers, then came home to have some more beers at night during dinner or watching TV at night. If we were going to barbeque at home, my dad would be the one that would grill everything, with a Falstaff beer to two. Otherwise, it was up to my mom to make sure dinner was on.

I never thought about why my mother never barbequed, as it was always my dad that took care of that. Barbeque really was not my thing, although I ate it. I did not like the texture of eating gristle, and I did not like charred meat, (still don't like either) both of which were there on occasion. I just knew it was his chance to sit there with a beer or two and relax, and it was his role. My mom's role was to cook dinner, or the rest of dinner if it was barbeque. Also, she had other things she did like make lunches, and breakfast, which tended to be pop tarts, or cereal, or something that we could do ourselves once we got old enough. All of the laundry, grocery and clothes shopping was my mom's bailiwick, along with paying the bills, cleaning the house, vacuuming, mopping, washing dishes nightly, signing permission slips for school, attending teacher's conferences, doing all of the banking which required actually going to the bank in those days since there was no such thing as online banking or ATM's, and a whole lot of other things I cannot think of at the moment. Oh yeah, she had a job of her own starting around my sixth grade year, which started as part time and moved to full time when I reached eighth grade. While they seemed to share the jobs of driving us to practices, my mom took us to every doctor, dentist, and orthodontist appointment.

Now my mom really ran the house, keeping everything up. She woke up early to get things done, starting with laundry daily and making lunches for us and for my dad. She made sure we were busy with something either in or outside of the house, and if not, making sure that we were outside playing with friends in the neighborhood. It did not take long to know who was in charge, the answer to that was obviously my dad.

Yes, my dad appeared in charge. At least that is how I saw it. You see, my dad was then one who went to work, and made the money. If we acted up at all, the threat would be, "Just wait until your dad gets home!" He would tell her what he had scheduled and she reacted accordingly. These dynamics did allow my mom to have power, but she was the one that we saw working, which as younger kids, we took for granted. We were assigned duties as we got older (dog poop in the back yard and cleaning the toilet were the two of mine that I can easily recall), but she continued to worry about everyone and their needs often with her own needs coming last. If we went on any kind of trip or vacation, it was always my mom that made the reservations. The gender roles were clearly defined.

There was more. As the first born boy, I was told at an early age that I would be going to college, and that I needed to get good grades to do it. When I was a young guy, before school age, I mentioned to my dad that I wanted to be a bricklayer, like he was, when I grew up. He said, "No, no way. You are going to college and get a job where you make more money and don't have to work so hard." So that was that, which was fine, I really did not know exactly what a bricklayer did in those days; it was later in my high school years that I worked with him on his side jobs. But as time went along and I realized I wanted to be a professional hockey player, *and* for some reason, I wanted to be like my mom. Why? I still had no idea. I knew I could not be like my mom because, well, that is just not the way it is for boys. That did not stop me from wanting to be pretty like her, and wear the clothes she wore. It was the endless chores that did not look very fun that she was doing that I was not sure I wanted to sign on to.

For years I felt this way, but had no idea why I was confused about which path I wanted: be a pro hockey player or my mom or any of the women on television. I already deduced as a first grader that I had a free pass from working too much around the house since, you know, I was born a boy, and that seemed to be the way it was. My friends' parents had the same type of roles, and it was just the way it was as well. More and more confusion crept inside my brain, and I knew beyond a shadow of a doubt that I could not reveal this little secret. All of this somehow added to my little secret from a few years earlier with the Superman/Lois Lane dilemma, and seemed to make sense that it should find its own little spot in the vault. I also figured if I was like my mom, I would also be expected to grow up and do everything like she did around the house, which made the entire thing a bit less attractive.

This vault I am talking about was definitely someplace in my head from the very time I realized I did not feel like other boys. I would live here with my stored information that MUST stay there, but at the same time, a place where my real person existed. Not lived in, just existed. The metaphor 'the closet' was not within the vernacular in those days, at least in my world. A closet never even had a lock on it, and we would hide in there from each other, but it was some place we could go and hide but come out of freely. I knew what I needed was definitely a vault, a place I walked into and could stand around in, and get locked in, like what happened in cartoons, or on Superman. It was a place that a person could not get out of, no one having the combination to, and that only

Superman could break me out of. There was no doubt that this is where these thoughts needed to go, and that is where they indeed went. From a young age, I appreciated my mom's sense of style and the way she presented herself. As I moved through middle school and high school, she was in her thirties to early forties. During those pivotal years, I frequently heard adults and peers alike remarking on how gorgeous and beautiful she was. Her physical attractiveness was undeniable, and these compliments only reinforced my admiration for her. She was my mother, so I did not look at her quite in that way, but I knew she loved me, and as I got older she began to talk to me more as an adult. I began to see her as a beautiful woman, and I was also secretly glad when people would make comments about how much I looked like her. In my middle school, people would comment that I looked like my mom, which I rejected out loud since I did not realize people were not implying that I looked like a girl but that I had similar features to her, however I secretly celebrated these comments. My self-imposed incarceration inside the heavy vault sitting on top of my shoulders, where my brain is, will keep things as the status quo on the outside as I pursue my hockey dream. My mom worked hard to keep her weight down, as she was always dieting, and ate little for breakfast and lunch, and ate salads for dinner. It was a lot of work on her part to make herself look great and feel great. Did it pay off? For the time being, it did. But for absolute certainty, things will remain status quo on the outside as I pursue my hockey dream.

Dealing with my brothers was somewhat typical. My middle brother, Grant, could not have been more different from me. I had blonde hair, he had coal black hair. My looks resembled my mother's, while his resembled my father's. He liked bikes, and as he got older, he liked the idea of fixing them, and he learned what he could about them. In his upper teenage years, he was into cars, and fixing them, taking things apart and putting them back together. I liked playing sports, and as I got older, my passion for playing sports grew even stronger. Grant dropped out of sports, did not take school all that seriously, and went to a technical high school to learn a trade, which for him was auto mechanics. I knew I was going to college to play hockey, and did what I had to do to get B's and A's in school. He started smoking cigarettes a bit when we got older, but I took better care of myself in order to be at my top condition for hockey. I had a plan, and I had no time for anything that would ruin my plan.

My younger brother, Darren, was more like me, as far as interests and personality. He in some ways was my little clone, who loved hockey and played the same sports as I did, right down to playing goalie in hockey, just like I did. We thought it was cool, to the chagrin of our parents, who had to foot the bill for two sets of expensive goalie equipment, which was significantly more expensive than the other players. We typically played with used equipment, and he often used my hand-me downs, just like we would do with clothes. He would play with us every day outside growing up, although the kids would be significantly older, that never seemed to matter, he was always tough enough to hang with the older kids and compete. Once he became old enough to play with us, he was the youngest and was the one stuck in the goalie position during the street hockey games, which worked since he was a good athlete and could handle it. He was my partner playing catch at home or whenever we went someplace, either to a Sunday afternoon antique auction, to a cousin's house, anywhere where we could play catch, and turn it into baseball skill-related games. Grant would join us on occasion, but he was not really interested and sort of did his own thing by himself.

For the most part, Darren and I were rather close with a lot to talk about, leaving Grant on his own a bit, with very little in common. This led to some sort of animosity, which led to arguments and fights between Grant and I. I had the upper hand for a while, but that changed as he got to be about as large or larger than I was, and could kick my butt. I had to do a lot of avoiding, but we were always in close proximity and we just did not get along. My mom would not want to leave us alone together in the middle and high school years, for fear that we would hurt each other. This was a smart idea, and it worked to my advantage, since she would take the younger two on errands, leaving me home by myself. This could not have worked out better for me.

4

WHO WAS MOVING UP?

OUR HOUSE HAD TWO BEDROOMS, AN EAT-IN KITCHEN, and a living room, all of them decent sized. We had a full basement that was used for the washer and dryer, a furnace room, and a large main room with a stereo, a fireplace that dad would barbeque in during the winter months, and a bar area with a lot of lights. It had its own entrance and our parents hosted a couple of parties down there when we were younger, but it turned out that as we grew older, the main area was always cluttered and used more as storage, and most importantly, our hockey equipment.

My brothers Grant and Darren and I shared the same small, thirteen foot by thirteen foot room since we were little, and by the time I reached eighth grade, it was simply too small and problematic as we all were growing. We also developed different interests, and a greater need for privacy. This necessitated my parents to remodel the attic into a large bedroom for the three of us. I say large, I mean it was significantly larger than the one we were in, utilizing all of the walking space in the attic. The attic had a slanted ceiling on both sides which limited the walking space, but the floor space was much more, so we liked it a lot.

This was an awesome change! I did not have my own room, but I had my own section, which was enough of a barrier that they had to stay out of. Even as we shared a room, the arrangement necessitated me to walk through their area to get to my space. The privacy was not completely there, since there was only a 6 foot long wall on one side of the attic as a boundary, and handmade wood bookcases with no back on them on the other side, leaving a 5 foot opening to get into my area, and full vision of each other.

While there was not a lot of privacy when everyone was home, I was old enough, and independent enough, to stay at home by myself rather than get in the car every time my mom had to go to a store or run some other errand. When this happened and my brothers went with her, I had my chance. I would use the time by myself at home to go into the attic which was by now my room, and had a need to dress up in my mother's old clothes that were stored behind a small door in the attic. I had no idea where this need to do this came from, but with the door leading from my room to behind the wall to where she stored her old dresses that she no longer wore, I had to take advantage of this gift.

Did you hear that? The very clothes I wanted to wear but could never wear, were literally in the closet in my room? Whenever possible, I would wear some of these older dresses then go downstairs into her actual closet and try on shoes. I would practice walking in them, gradually leading up to wearing them for the entire time she was gone, and going all through the house. These were special times for me, although I did not know why at the time. It just felt natural. I would stare at myself in the mirror in my parents room for a long time in different poses, or what I thought were poses. I had no idea how to walk or act as a woman, I just knew I loved the warm, relaxed and somewhat anxious feeling I had. Oftentimes I could not take my eyes off of that mirror, and I totally loved the person I saw. Our house had a gravel driveway, so I could hear when the car drove in and was back home. I had roughly 20 seconds to nervously tear everything off, run upstairs to hide everything or place them in the exact place that I found them, and hang out in my room or play with the dogs to make it look like I was just doing normal boy things. The need to present "normal" again made me feel a bit dejected for reasons I did not fully understand at the time, but that feeling set in after the anxious mad dash to replace all items to where to belong as to not leave a shred of evidence that this secret activity was happening.

The sharing a room business lasted until I reached high school, when we were fighting almost all the time, and needed our own space. I lobbied my parents hard for the room downstairs to myself with the other two sharing the upstairs, since I was the oldest, and I was playing a higher level of hockey at this point and needed time to do my own thing to get ready for games, particularly the Junior B games and the high school games. The late hours for practices, combined with my work at the rink, made it essential for me to have my own space. I ultimately won this argument, enjoying the privacy I craved along with a greater sense of autonomy.

Around this time, I was dying to have a girlfriend, but was too shy to ask anyone out. I was attracted to girls, but also pictured myself wearing their clothes and living their lives. I did not know what was happening, but I knew not to tell anyone that I actually wanted to be the girlfriend, or my life would significantly change for the uncomfortable and worse. I began to hang around my dad as I was required to go to work with him to some of his small jobs and help mix mortar and carry bricks. He worked with other men, all of which had the same attitudes as my father did, with the women being at home taking care of things, having dinner ready, and getting things done, such as paying the bills. This seemed to be the prevailing theme among his co-workers, and the other parents that he hung out with as he coached soccer and baseball for my brother's teams. Everywhere I looked, and from every direction I had heard from, it was dead obvious: the men set the rules.

That was true everywhere you looked. The men were the bosses, and if the women actually worked outside the home, it was predominantly an entry level position. They were teachers and nurses, but not the principal or doctor who had the final say.

It was also evident at the family gatherings at my father's parent's house, where almost the entire family of my father's five sisters and one brother, with 18 cousins. Anytime a kid needed a diaper change, or a younger kid needed anything, not one of the men drinking in the kitchen would think to put their cigarette down and help with the kid, it was always the mother's job. They had to spend their time in the kitchen talking about their "old ladies," and other wife jokes, that they could not be bothered to look after their own kid. Without ever hearing the words before I realized it was a man's world, and I saw no other option but to take my rightful place in it.

During those years, I was starting to take hockey very seriously. I had my heart set on attending Vianney High School, a private Catholic all-boys school, with the hope of playing hockey for them. I was doing everything I could to excel at the sport, and I knew I also needed to maintain good grades and pass an entrance exam to gain acceptance.

In school, I spent my time drawing team logos in my notebooks, on scraps of paper, and on book covers. I was completely consumed by hockey. I not only attended practices and games but also made my way to public skating sessions to skate and socialize, well, sort of. It depended on the day.

Back then, ADHD wasn't widely recognized or talked about, and I don't remember it being diagnosed. But I had it; I needed to move constantly. This made it difficult for me to approach girls. I had crushes, but my shyness and lack of familiarity with the social scene my peers were involved in held me back. Who was I, after all?

The one thing I knew for certain was that I wanted to be a

college and professional hockey goalie. That ambition drove me, even as all these other challenges loomed around me, coming at me at a rapid pace.

This confusion remained right where it belonged, in the vault.

5
OPPORTUNITIES GAINED, OPPORTUNITIES LOST

IF I WAS SHY AND DID NOT KNOW WHAT TO DO WITH OR say to girls in the middle school years, I was painfully shy around girls in high school. I knew I did not have any clue, or confidence to be with a girl, let alone what to do with or say to someone I was crushing on beyond "hi." I was awkward and terrified.

I actually had a couple of short-lived girlfriends, those who I met at the rink where my team played. Both were figure skaters that skated at the Brentwood Ice Rink. The only reason I went out with them is because they liked me first, and I only knew that because some of the other kids my age that worked at the rink told me. We had the rink in common, and our love for the ice, which made the conversations a bit easier to start. I got to know them a bit, and we held hands and kissed, and nothing else. I was really afraid to let them meet my parents. I was embarrassed for some reason. I could not really understand why, but was not comfortable about how my mom would react. Make too big of a deal, embarrass me, I did not know, but I knew that my parents meeting her was off the table. I was not in love, but it did feel good to kiss someone and hold hands. Neither relationship lasted more than two to three weeks tops.

I had also spent a lot of time with my 16-U hockey coach, who was short, heavy, single, the youngest of eight kids, never married, no kids of his own, did not have a car and lived alone. He was very good to me, finding me all kinds of ice time, which is what I was looking for, and was on my side as one of my coaches that was trying to get me a college opportunity. I was driving as soon as I turned sixteen, but before that, I would often play a game, then spend the night at his house to be able to go to practice or game the next morning. Since my parents had my two other brothers that had to go places, it made the ride situation easier for my parents.

Spending the night meant a lot of things. Most often, it involved raunchy porno movies, made convenient by his brother owning a video store and his access to any amount of videos he wanted. As a teen boy with a fear of relationships with girls, to be able to be at his place and masturbate away to porn videos was just about the next thing to perfect, other than the ability to dress up to that same teen girl. As close as I got was to wear a pair of women's panties, provided by said coach, luckily they fit, although I never really knew whose they were to begin with, who would have left them there. And why were they there in the first place? He got possessive, to the point if I wanted to try to go to a high school party with one of my teams, he would not let me, even to the point of him threatening to invite a different player over. Sexual expectations became more frequent as time went along. It was more of a relationship than I was looking for. He groomed me, subtly manipulating my vulnerabilities. My fear of social situations, my confusion about my sexuality, and my longing for acceptance all played into his hands. The line between mentorship and exploitation blurred, and I found myself entangled in a relationship that was both confusing and damaging, but I stayed away from drinking and the drug scene with the rest of my teammates from my three hockey teams that way, and did not have to be put in uncomfortable positions with being around a bunch of people, girls included, and me having such a hard time talking to any of them.

The other uncomfortable situation was being in the same bed with a grown man and asked to do things I had never seen before. This was insane at first, but the uncomfortable feelings subsided a bit as time went along. Despite it becoming more normal for me, it did not feel right, not at all. But to tell anyone about this situation would in my mind mean outing myself, but for what, I did not know. I did not give a single thought about what would happen to him, but I was worried about what my parents would think, and did not want to hurt them, to let them down. Male genitalia did absolutely nothing for me, in fact it was repulsive. I knew intrinsically that I was so rooted inside the vault since I was more concerned about getting rides to hockey, having some sort of independence and keeping me out of awkward social situations than realizing I was being molested. For my parents and all those who knew me to find out who I truly was deep down was much worse in my mind than being sexually assaulted from one of my coaches. The confines of the vault would keep me safe with my secrets yet was so damaging at the same time. These episodes did not happen often, and when it did the positives seemed to outweigh the negatives, and at least rides were easier to work out for practice the next day along with the avoidance of social situations. It definitely supplied quite a bit more material for my vault, and would not dare utter a word of this for so many reasons, mainly the negative stigma that would affect the social status that I had along with. I felt that I may need to build shelves to organize everything that went on in there on a regular basis.

Other than this scenario, another reason I was not completely into the idea of a "girlfriend" was because I had a rather large, overwhelmingly strong crush on a girl that worked at the Brentwood Rink. Darlene was a year older than me in school, short and as cute as could be. I hung out at the rink a lot, it was easier and more comfortable than trying to make other friends that were my age and I could stay away from the party scene that happened with high school parties. I did not like the taste of beer, and would not take my first sip until the end of my second collegiate hockey season.

Darlene and I became friends. She was such a friendly soul, and I valued her friendship. In the same sort of way I was living the dichotomy of being attracted to girls at the same time as wanting to be a girl, she was both a good friend, a person that I enjoyed talking to yet also I had such a blinding crush on her. Yet I could not bring myself to tell her how I felt. I felt I was good at being a friend, but two things were at play; it would kill me to ruin a friendship by asking her out, which I didn't even know how to do, and screw it up so badly. The other was I was scared to death of showing her a tremendously awkward side of me, risking her rejecting me, and accusing me of taking advantage of our friend-ship to get to her. Also, did I want to be just like her? Did I want to be her boyfriend or girlfriend? I wanted to be her boyfriend, and possibly her husband someday, but something inside me was telling myself that I wanted to someday be her girlfriend instead, whatever that meant since same-sex marriage was not legal and the whole thing was unbelievably confusing. I had not even consid-ered the possibility of being her girlfriend, or anyone's girlfriend in my world back then with virtually no role models. In my final analysis, I knew being her friend was one way to enjoy her company, and I did not want to lose one of the few real good friends I had at that time. It drove me crazy when she began to date people that I knew, and really bugged me when she dated a guy that I did not like, one that I knew was no good for her. I knew it was useless to try to talk her out of it, and I was her friend none-theless. My love for her was unconditional. She was the nicest person to me and I would not do anything to jeopardize that.

All of this confusion really messed with my confidence socially with peers, and the one place I felt comfortable was at the rink, and playing hockey. I was even getting into coaching younger kids in hockey, helping a couple of younger goalies out at their practices. Hockey was not only my passion but my refuge. I knew hockey would bring me out of my shell, or whatever it was holding me back socially, and I felt confident within myself totally when playing hockey and at a rink. I knew I wanted to be a coach when I grew up, after, of course, being a college and pro goalie. I loved playing goalie, stopping pucks, frustrating shooters, helping teammates by talking and constantly communicating on the ice about where to pass, who to cover, and where the pass is going, among other things. I felt like a coach on the ice, and I felt like I needed to be a coach on the ice. I was able to use my voice, and also let my play speak for itself, things I did not necessarily have confidence in off the ice. This learning environment and coaching type of experience made me realize I wanted to be part of the game in some form or fashion for my life, that I could be successful with this as a profession, although I did not completely understand exactly what goes into coaching for a living. I couldn't consider any other profession that did not include coaching or teaching. I found my calling there.

All through my high school years, I worked at the ice rink that I had grown up in, Affton Ice Rink. I was an Assistant Manager as soon as I obtained my driver's license and I was eligible for driving the Zamboni. I would be in charge of operations on nights, I worked on Wednesday nights, the only night that did not conflict with hockey games and practices. I would also work weekends, either opening the building, which I loved, or closing the building, which I liked. From sixteen to eighteen, I was responsible for managing a busy building full of students, parents, and others; an experience that gave me real-world leadership skills, great part-time pay, and the confidence to communicate with people of all ages. It was a formative and unforgettable part of growing up. I felt at home working at the rink I pretty much grew up in, and $5.00/hr was great money in 1981-83. I took as many hours as I could get, as many as I was available for. All other nights and days, I found myself at the rink playing a game, which I loved, along with practicing and hanging out at Brentwood Rink, the home of my junior team, The Blazers, because that is where Darlene was working. These rinks were my comfort zones, my happy places.

By the end of my hockey seasons of my senior year in high school, March, 1983, I had a strong high school season and made the High School All Star game played at the St. Louis Arena. I was playing really well for my junior team at the same time, and the Jr. B National Tournament happened to be in St. Louis. Our team made it, and I had an outstanding tournament. Once we were eliminated, a couple of college coaches spoke with me about going to take a look at their school. The same day, Don Lumley, coach at Kent State University cornered me and said he is absolutely looking for a goalie and would love for me to take a look. He offered me a partial scholarship right there on the spot, and after a campus visit I committed to Kent State University. It offered a beautiful campus, large student body, far from home, a chance for me to spread my wings, tons of possibilities, and most importantly, they needed a goalie for their Division I independent program and they wanted me to be that guy. There were a couple of St. Louis area players on the team, and that made it easy to adjust and to get information. I fell in love with the entire idea and could not wait to get there.

For the remainder of the school year, still without a girlfriend, prom came and went without me. I know my parents spent a ton of money for my hockey habit, and did not want to spend a lot of money for an event that I did not want to be at. I could not dance, I mean at all, and had no confidence to even try it nor to be in any other uncomfortable social circumstance. I refused to do any dancing, or be involved in any activity that was considered the least bit feminine. I would never put myself in a situation that would give anyone the chance to think I was gay, or queer, or anything except a good goalie. I figured I would worry about girls when I start over in college. I threw myself into the preparation for hockey and school, and working as much as possible at the rink and umpiring baseball and softball. Darlene and I did not see each other as much, she had other interests, but more importantly, no time since I had worked so much and skated a lot during summer hockey preparing for college hockey.

The last time I saw Darlene was the night before I was leaving for college. She drove my 16U coach over to Affton Rink where I was working to spend a bit of time and to say goodbye. I was close to both of them, and it was awesome to see Darlene after not seeing her in a couple of months it seemed, my heart nearly melted on the spot. Around closing, she was helping me clean up, and my coach left us alone in the lobby. I had no idea what it was but I had amazing feelings, not knowing what they were or why, but whatever they were they were raging all around us. How do I do this? Do I tell her? If so, do I stay in touch? Screw it, I could not help it, I decided right then and there I would say something. What I would say, I had no idea. Just then, she approached me with her body right next to me and looked up at me with her beautiful soft eyes. We hugged slowly and kissed for what seemed like 10 minutes before coming up for air. We sat down and then lounged on the floor, just looking at each other, being with each other, and kissing. Up to this point in my life, I had never felt anywhere close to this, absolutely nothing like it. The feelings I felt were conflicted; I was experiencing the best feeling I had ever felt with the girl that I had the most feelings for up to that point, and now it was ok to act on those feelings. At the same time, I was so pissed at myself for not acting on my emotions long before that.

After our first kiss came our first fight. She was also upset at me, asking, "Why didn't you ever say anything before? I can't believe you!"

For ten extremely awkward seconds or so, which felt like five minutes of silence, I had no reply, other than saying, "I have always felt this way," then stammered something like "I am too shy and did not want to be embarrassed about liking you because I figured you would not like me like that because I am not in your league."

She initiated another long kiss, I found some confidence and said, "You could have said something to me."

"How did you not know?"

"I had no idea, how would I know that?" I had absolutely no idea how this whole thing worked, so this time it was my turn to initiate a kiss and avoid awkwardness.

This entire experience was very special and awkward for me, and for us, but I was so incredibly thrilled like I had never been before, and was suddenly confident that the cutest and nicest girl in my world, the perfect girl and person to be in love with was actually crushing on me. Our hugging lasted a long time, and I remember fighting back tears as she was crying at finally saying goodbye. I felt on top of the world and completely empty at the same time. It would not be the last time I had opposite feelings at the same time, although for other reasons.

During the summer after my freshman year of college, I had heard that Darlene was married to a professional wrestler. I had not heard from her, and that is the life she created for herself for the past year or two and I was happy for her.

Kind of. I was terribly disappointed at the same time. Even though I had a girlfriend at college at this time, I was still pissed at myself, really pissed that I did not say anything sooner. I could do nothing about that, but I was heartbroken. I was not the least bit mad at her at all, I understood the situation completely. This was on me, and I felt I could not tell anyone about this for I sensed that feeling bad about losing a girl would make me look weak, and that would spiral into a huge outcast of me by every single dude I know. As if that made any difference, I continued to take all of my feelings I felt inside the vault into consideration when deciding how to handle emotional situations. I took care of it like I took care of everything else. I could not tell anyone about it. I found its own spot in the vault and told no one about these feelings.

Decades later, we connected on facebook and would message each other for quite a long time. I messaged her and we began to communicate for a few months. One day I asked her to talk and gave her my phone number, as I could not continue to write messages to one another. We spoke by phone for about three hours. It was awesome to catch up, and we continued to communicate. It was very nice, even though we moved on in many ways since those days, it was so refreshing to be able to reconnect with the first person who I was in love with, and re-establish a loving friendship. As Darlene would say often, we met as kids, and loved one another, and we will have love for each other forever, one that will not go away. I concur completely. Neither of us were looking for another relationship at that moment, and it is fulfilling to have one of my best friends back.

6

REBRANDING

OTHER THAN MY HOCKEY ABILITY, MY ENTHUSIASM FOR playing the game and excitement of being away on my own, most everything from home in St. Louis was suppressed. I forgot about my coach and put Darlene into the background, as difficult as it was to tuck away the memory of our last meeting. I was somehow laser focused on my new and exciting life ahead, something I had dreamed about constantly and worked hard toward, which would be as a college goalie, then, who knows what from there.

Moving for college 11 hours away from home accelerated the moving on process and I had not heard from her, but that is the life she immersed herself into and I was happy for her and terribly disappointed at the same time. And for a brief time pissed at myself.

I met a girl within a couple of weeks at Kent, and dated her throughout my freshman year. We did not have sex the entire year. I tried too hard to bring her around to my idea of a lifestyle, no drinking or smoking, and being together all the time. I wrote letters pretty much every week during the summer and was greatly anticipating seeing her the following year when she would be living in my dorm. It turned out I was too controlling, likely mimicking a 'role model' from the previous few years, and she rightfully dumped me at the beginning of my sophomore year. So after I collected everything back, like my high school jacket, and high school ring, and other items, I moved on and dated different girls for a little bit, none of them seemed to work out for a long period of time. But I enjoyed meeting people, loved growing up and getting comfortable inside my own skin, and was relieved while realizing for the first time that girls just might be attracted to me. This was great, because I was, and am still, attracted to women. Maybe I am 'normal' after all, maybe I do fit in with the rest of the guys?

College was an amazing and invigorating growing up process for me. I had the opportunity to explore who I really was, what I wanted to do for the rest of my life, and who I would possibly do it with. I loved it, met so many amazing people, and learned so many things, both academically and socially. As a player on the hockey team, certain things were easier to do, such as get into bars while I was not of age to do so. One popular bar in Kent, the Crazy Horse, was a large dance club and was operated by sports fans, and in particular, hockey fans. The team doctor, who also happened to be the bouncer, would check ID's at the door, always allowing the athletes in without any cover charge collected. The General Manager of the bar would go to the games, oftentimes taking pictures from the penalty box. I was stunned my first night there when he approached me, told me he loves watching the games and me play, and asked if he could get me a drink. I did not drink at that time, but the offer seemed to stand for the rest of the time that the bar was around, especially with a teammate working there as a bartender. This increase of social life made it easier to befriend athletes from other teams, which I took advantage of.

Once the Horse went out of business, it was Ray's Place, which was a drinking bar which is still a Kent institution, brightly lit with music that was different that any I had ever heard before, but I really grew to love. Reggae music was new to me, as was that of the Talking Heads. Songs that were not country or pop music like I was exposed to in the past, or the dance music that blared at the other bars and that I shied away from, due to my inability to and my disinterest in dancing. This atmosphere made Ray's my favorite, not only because of the atmosphere and that it was the most popular bar in Kent, but also because of the wide range of people that would be there. There would be predominately students, athletes, but also others from town, and some from what appeared to be "alternative lifestyles." Somehow, without realizing it at the time, I felt more comfortable around a diverse crowd. Although I could not verbalize what diversity was, I felt at home here.

I met a girl at the beginning of junior year, and dated for three years. We got along well, and yet I was still focused on work and hockey, and still wanted to get a chance for a pro hockey tryout after college. It was as long as I had ever dated anyone up to that point, and we actually got engaged in the middle of my senior year. It seemed like the thing to do, the natural next step. She was supportive of me, and with her being a junior when I graduated and that I had to stay an extra year to student-teach and ended up as an assistant coach on the local high school team, whose home ice was right there in the rink in which I played. It was perfect, even being able to land an entry level job at the rink to work with programming. I'm not sure I recall exactly what my title was or what I was supposed to do, but I was essentially the assistant manager. I had hours, and had to make sure the students showed up for work. I do not remember much about that job, honestly, but I was being paid, put on a few hockey clinics in the spring, and I was still there to be around my girlfriend while she finished her undergrad. By the end of her senior year, I could sense we were growing apart. I was either not ready for marriage, or not ready to spend the rest of my life with her, or with anyone, or both, or perhaps something completely different that I had not yet figured out but it had something that was very quietly scurrying sound in the corner of the vault, seemingly getting a bit restless after a five-year hibernation.

I visited her at her summer internship at a mid-atlantic beach town, where things just did not go well and we basically broke it off right there. I had a feeling I was not ready. The fact that we used her mother's diamond for the engagement ring, kind of made it an easy exit if I ever needed it, which honestly may have been my plan all along. I liked the idea of attachment, and having a loving soul with me at all times, but not sure of a commitment for the rest of my life at that point. No idea why, it just wasn't there, and I was not proud of myself for taking it to that level with the key to the escape hatch in my possession. I actually felt awful about the way I handled the breakup.

During college, my urges to possibly become a girlfriend or even a bride were substantially suppressed. I was coming out of my awkward shell, being more comfortable with girls, and crowds at bars and parties, but most importantly, friends. Once in a great while, in private, I would sneak into a friend's roommate's closet and try on her flats. It wasn't about her, it was about carving out a sliver of space that felt true to me. About three times in two years. That was it. That was the extent of my dressing up, or even thinking about anything I used to think about. Perhaps everything was going away and I was getting to "normal?" Done with puberty and had my act together? Maybe, maybe not. I knew I liked who I was becoming and growing into, or at least fitting in like a normal-ish straight guy, and did not want anything to screw that up. For these and other extremely important reasons, I just committed to never figuring out the magic password to open the door of the vault, realizing I needed to actively keep this where it was, which was away from absolutely everyone in the whole wide world. I knew I had to do what I could to stay clear of ideas or people who could possibly trigger me right back to the other person and hoist that vault right back on my shoulders.

7

THE REASON I WAS THERE

HONESTLY, BESIDES THE ABUSE I WOULD RECEIVE IF I would somehow come out and act on all of my imprisoned feelings, the other main reason for this suppression of this major feeling that has accompanied my mind and body since I was five years old was that I was playing college hockey. I was right where I had dreamed I would someday be. There was no way I was going to screw this up with a lack of focus and discipline, and I did not want to waste a single game sitting on the bench. I had anywhere from 20-25 teammates at any given time in the same locker room and shower area. Everyone knows a lot about each other when you spend each day with the same group of guys, let alone be naked at times with all of those guys on a daily basis in the shower area and such. Lots of stories are shared in there, tons of teasing and busting on each other about what they were doing on recent nights and who they were doing it with. I was also always pushing myself against the talented competition for playing time in goal. I was there to play hockey, I was driven to be the starting goaltender, and that is what I was going to do. Nothing within my control was going to derail this dream, especially something playing with my head that would not only jeopardize my place on the team and my stature as a teammate, not to mention my overall safety and well being. The embarrassment of the entire campus and possibly the entire hockey world, my parents, everyone I know and have ever met, and what felt like the entire world was a huge motivator to keep the vault tightly closed for good and never even try to escape this privacy. Taking chances, or even going near a possible chance to be discovered, was not going to happen; I was having the time of my life during those years, including living at school while working during the summers for my remaining three years of college, thus ending my residence in Affton, Missouri.

This piece cannot be understated. I literally lived for this. No matter what my name was, or who I dated, or who I thought I would become, or whatever friends I had and what their idea of fun happened to be, I was first and foremost a goalie on the Kent State Golden Flashes. I did not drink a drop of alcohol until after my sophomore hockey season, I mean not at all. My friends that I had at the time were fine with that, and it was not long until I tried drinking and joined in and became a more regular college student, and I had fun doing it like most everyone else did. I was very good about not going out during the week during the season, and was smart about how much I did on Saturday nights. After the season was the time to catch up on whatever downtown Kent had to offer, like Hot Legs contests (think of a beauty/popularity contest), the Drink and Drown promotions, and the rest of the buffoonery that goes on in a college town.

But it was the day to day part of the season I lived for. I knew I needed to show up and bring it every day at practice. There was only one net in the games and room for only one goalie at a time, and there were one to three other guys besides me that wanted to be in it, and deserved to be. I lived for the opportunity to go to the rink, and compete for playing time, along with working hard to build a program. Our program was Division I Independent at the time, and was only a few years old as a varsity team, after a decade of success as a club program. Our schedule had improved through the four years that I had played there, with us joining a league by our senior season. There were rumors about us looking to join the CCHA, the premier division I league at the time, but that was a distant future to us, no player on the roster that I played with was on the team that eventually joined that league. It was the competition day to day that made the entire experience worth it, and competing with countless other goalies, with two of them, Ernie and Dan, becoming two of my best friends. It was a healthy competition, and I was fortunate to have the many goalie partners that were supportive to whoever was in the net. Everyone wanted to play, but there was support from all of us for the night's starter. Looking back, out of nine players in our recruiting class, only two of us played all four years. Our recruiting class was actually among the smallest of any during the time that I was there, meaning the coaches were constantly trying to upgrade the talent each year. This is at a level where no spot is guaranteed, and the players that give the team the best chance to win will get the opportunities to play. As a goalie, I knew that there is always a partner or more that was there to be the starter, and it was always my goal to outwork everyone on the ice, and do what I could to help the team win. I realize the competition within the team is a critical part of it, and I worked hard to make sure I earned the one goalie spot in the net come game time.

Game days were sacred. The night before games, I went with a few of the guys to a local restaurant for a meal the evening prior to game night. These games were huge, especially home games. Hockey was the only sport that the students had to pay admission to attend games on campus, and the rink was crowded. You knew it was game night when you smelled popcorn and hot dogs when we walked into the building. The rink held around 1,700 fans, so it was intimate and loud. It was a lot of fun to be in there, and I never took it for granted.

That is not to say I was on every single night. Early on in my freshman season, Coach Lumley and his wife Elaine, made a deal with us that the team would get a steak dinner at their house if we swept Penn State, a long-time rival. The first game of the series was televised locally, and I gave up three early goals. Coach Lumley called a time out, brought the team over, which coaches usually do to reset the team and get back on track. Instead of dealing with the team, he looked directly at me and told me in a very stern voice "Bear Down!" He went on to say other things, and once I realized this time out was because of me not being ready or focused, the adrenaline began to run through me and I do not remember a thing he said past that. Coach Lumley was the coach who recruited me to Kent and gave me this incredible opportunity, and I am out here letting him down, and letting the team down with it. I shut them down from then on, we swept the series, and had a night with the team at the Lumley's house for a steak dinner and to watch the replay of the telecast of the game on TV. It was rare in the early to mid-eighties to have one of our games televised, even on local close circuit TV. It was neat to see, and I also remembered that night as one where my job was on the line, and I would not let him, the team, or myself down again by just not being ready. It was a huge wake up call, as it was a little bit into our season, a bit past the pure excitement and euphoria of the first few games, where the adrenaline was automatically flowing. I had other suspect performances in my career, but never because I was not prepared.

With all of this going on in college, I was not about to throw all of this away for something sitting in the vault that I was not aware could ever happen, especially when that something was so nebulous that I could not even wrap my arms around what exactly it was. Also, whatever that something was, it was considered very wrong by what seemed like everyone in our society.

Wrong? Yes, wrong. More and more, the older I got, the messages never changed. Every message I had ever received, either directly or indirectly, indicated that anything queer was wrong. Gay kids were picked on at school in high school, and suspicion of queer in any way got you picked on in the middle school grades. Early in my freshman year I happened to be with a few people from a class walking through the student center, when one of the older guys said, "Look, see that guy over there, he is in charge of the Gay organization on Campus," to which another one of the group blurts out, "Yeah, he's the chief fag."

Ok, that was about a couple of weeks into my freshman year, but that was just about enough for me to know the vault will remain sealed tight. But if that was not enough, there was plenty of reinforcement being around two dozen or more athletes, many of which are continually establishing a leadership hierarchy, including the initiations of rookies. The older players shaved the freshman's heads, attempting to be in a Mohawk. Mine was a mess, some of the guys were more of a mess than others. In the early 80's, the Mohawk style, or even short haircuts were not at all in style. Luckily, my girlfriend at the time was supportive and knew someone in her dorm who cut hair, so I went to her in desperation. She cleaned it up as much as she could but it still was uneven from side to side and front to back for the next few weeks until it grew back. Having her around was really a good thing at the time. I felt very vulnerable, and it was accentuated when my friend, a freshman on the women's swimming team, mentioned to me in class that she had just passed me on the way to class. I did not notice her at the time because I was walking with someone. She mentioned to me when we got to class that she passed a guy that she did not realize was me and thought to herself that "he would be really good looking if he had hair." When she told me this, I was not sure how to take that; I felt there was a compliment in there somewhere, but I read that to mean it was I was looking like some sort of creepy monster. I knew what she was trying to say and she was trying to make me feel better, but she said what she said.

Back to the queer thing, there were always remarks among the guys when an obvious feminine guy or a masculine girl walks by. I did not need to live on that side of the ledger at that point of my life. But perhaps nothing spelled it out like our dress code required from our new head coach at the beginning of my sophomore year. It was not written down, but announced in the locker room. When our captain asked what the dress code was, he replied, "Sport coats and ties, nothing faggot," (pause for effect-giggles and light laughter), "nothing faggot, no two-toned hair, no earrings."

Our coach was good at teaching hockey, knew the game, and we learned a lot about the game. He was a showman that loved to tell stories, some of them clearly embellished, and loved to be the funniest guy in the room. He was funny and brought a ton of energy and enthusiasm to the team, but comments like that were just another in a long line of comments I have heard from many players and most coaches fairly consistently as I got older. "Take your skirt off," "Hit him with your purse!" "Does your pussy hurt?" "You're playing like a bunch of fucking girls out there." These are said by both coaches and players alike, and there are plenty more examples, but you get the idea, none of which are particularly inviting to someone who may actually want to wear a skirt. Words matter.

I played goalie, a position that requires an incredible amount of mental toughness. The goalie is a huge part of the team, some of us will say the most important. When goals are scored against the goalie, the stat goes against the goalie. We know that hockey is more of a team game than that, but there is a whole host of other statistics just for goalies. We are separate, and most of the team has no idea how to play the position nor do they care, they just care that the goalies can stop the puck. We were also taught any show of weakness, being defeated, weak or not tough is a detriment to the goalie's success. The other team reads that, and will seize on that, doing everything they can to intimidate and to get the goalie off of their game. It was not acceptable to be weak or soft, and I felt that mattered off the ice as well, where the team needs to know the goalie can handle anything.

Words matter. Tone of voice matters. Even today, both in

athletics and in life in general, the term "Man up" is used quite a bit. If I as a coach am saying "man up" to a bunch of guys in the locker room on a regular basis, what is the message these guys are getting? What message could a female athletic trainer take? My take is that men are stronger than women. "Grow a pair" is another favorite. No one believes that "Grow a pair" means a pair of breasts. These messages say to a woman that to be strong and tough, and to lead any group with so much as a dude in it, you have to be a dude and have testicles, and you cannot play, behave, present like a woman, thus, stay down there on that second rung of the privilege ladder, if in fact you are cis and heterosexual.

How about the men? What message do they get? They get the same message, that in order to be strong and accomplish what you want you cannot play, behave or present like a woman, thus, you will sink down the privilege ladder where you belong while the tough dude takes what he feels is his rightful perch at the top of the pedestal. Ok, this is a generalization, but when a guy hears this over and over, he will believe it, and the misogynistic perception perpetuates.

An example of some of my experiences would be five to six guys having beers around a table. One of the guys makes a comment about what he is going to do sexually or physically, or both, to a girl that walks into the room. She could be a certain girl, or a girl he knows, or the girl over there, or any girl. One or two of the guys would chime in to say what they would do, often trying to eclipse the other one. A couple of the guys may or may not remain silent. What happens is that some of the guys would blow it off, thinking he is showing off. Some may think the guy who started it really likes the girl they are talking about. Yet there is someone in the crowd that believes he can do that to girls, that he deserves what he thinks the original guy is getting. Does he try it? Does the original guy or guys actually try what they say they were planning? It is my belief that this perception from a lifetime of toxic messages regarding what these guys are entitled to significantly exacerbates gender based misconduct.

While I have heard more than my share of these types of conversations, I rarely heard anyone ever ask the guy if the girl is at all interested in this, or if she should have any say in this plan. I guess it would be assumed that either the girl should not have a say in this plan, and that she has no input as to whether she agrees or not. The guy may or may not actually do, or intend to do, what he says he is going to do. The rest of the guys can giggle, and even make suggestions to make this encounter a little more interesting, or pile on for more humor. This is considered just locker room talk, or boys being boys, but hearing these messages over and over and over throughout a lifetime can indeed make it seem believable and ok. This talk is dangerous, and leads to scary things.

What would happen if someone steps up to say, "that is not a good idea, the girl should have a say in this," or something to mention this is wrong to do, that most of it violates the person in many ways, including illegal ways. I sat through many nights where I had beers with boys, and that talk always seems to come up in some form. Yes I heard it, yes, I sometimes participated in at least reinforcing this behavior and contributed to the conversation from time to time. I did not "grow a pair " and speak up against this type of talk and even the possibilities of following through on this fantasy. I did not do it in these situations, nor when the subject was about queers. I needed to fit in. The last thing I could afford, at least in my mind, was to be sensitive to any of these groups. I needed to fit in with the crowd to avoid being caught as one of the people they are in the process of ostracizing. Could I have prevented a sexual assault of any kind, simply by saying what someone else actually needs to hear, that the behavior being described is wrong? From an early age there are many ways that men are socialized to feel they are superior to women, that they are entitled to do what they want. I had no concept of this, and did not realize why this was the case since I, too, was socialized to believe the same thing. Somehow hearing a bunch of dudes talk about how they would treat the type of people that I thought I may or may not want to become made me take more notice. The more I noticed it, the more consternation occurred in my brain, since I felt that I would out myself if I were to defend a woman in that context, or women in general. So we can add this concept to the growing list of anxiety-inflaming situations.

Do I have any idea how I would know saying something contrary to the misogynistic talk could prevent a sexual assault? No, I do not have proof of this. I know I broke up at least two sexual assaults while they were happening at parties during my time in college, and I did not go to a large amount of parties in comparison to many of my friends and typical college students. One of the occasions, three guys were talking about all ganging up on a girl and "pulling a train" at the upcoming party at our house. A train on a girl meant all three of the guys would take their turn having sex with her. They attempted exactly what they talked about doing. I stopped them all, and they were pissed at me. I was blamed for them not being able to rape this girl after they got her drunk. These confrontations were in real time. I just reacted. I had no time to determine if they would be happy with me for getting in their way. The number of incidents are impossible to track, but suffice it to say that there are countless more incidents that happen than get reported, and of those that do, the number of cases that are brought to any type of adjudication is miniscule.

Perhaps some of the best actors are those with something to hide. People tend to hide these incidents they were victims of often without ever talking about them, ever, to anyone. This could often cause severe mental health issues. Those of us with something to hide would make great secret agents, we really learn how to keep a secret. I am positive that I would have been the best under-cover agent. I know I would have been because I was a double-agent for the largest portion of my life, with two different personas and names. The only thing missing was the fake ID. I am here to tell you that a queer person in the closet, or somewhere in their mind even more secure, could be the best at spying, knows best how to keep a secret, how to conceal an alias, and how to plan a visit somewhere that no one in their world would know about. I have absolutely no doubt about this. I am convinced. I did it for far too long to know that it works.

Here are four major ways that we as individuals and as a society can prevent the need to hide trauma or secrets about ourselves that I started to see in college, yet did not manifest until long after I graduated. First, we need to end the stigma of mental health needs, so people are comfortable getting help without being labeled. Mental health is as important to one's overall health and well-being as any other health concern. Honestly, conversations about mental health should be as frequent and normal as getting a haircut. Am I crazy that I see a therapist? No, but I would go crazy if I didn't.

Another way is to change our vernacular. We need more people to step up, be strong and call out insensitive language. We need to teach this to kids at an early age. Teachers, coaches, and any person of authority needs to alter their shtick a bit to create a more inclusive and inviting environment. We need to make it not cool to put others down, and particularly to see each other as equals. If you would not say something in front of a woman, either your spouse or loved one, or your mother, or children, do not say it in front of others that could hear it the wrong way. Do this whether you are talking to a specific person or talking about that specific person. Tough work? For some, maybe, but start with eliminating a phrase or a saying, one at a time. Find a way to lift someone up rather than tear someone down. Habits are difficult to break, but to eliminate one at a time is not a lot to ask, if you want to do it.

Third, teach this at an early age. This should be among the first things that kids experience. If they are indoctrinated into this at an early point in their life, they can know right from wrong early, so they do not have to de-program themselves like adults do, or like adults never get around to do. Stress to them that a black or brown kid is just as smart as the white kid is, that they have every bit of the right to be in space as the white kids do. Insist that school systems are teaching what really happened when the Europeans captured African people and enslaved them for generations. While you are at it, be sure they teach a comprehensive civics curriculum, with federal, state, and local governments. We live in democracy, so it is important that we know how democracy actually works, which will reinforce the need to treat black and brown, immigrant, LGBTQ+ people and women with respect and equality as anyone else. In a nutshell: End All Marginalization.

How did I get here, you ask, talking about how you can connect ending all marginalization of people from the phrase "Nothing Faggot?"

See the previous several paragraphs.

Fourth, and this is the most logical and obvious: Do not violate a woman, or a man, or anyone because you have absolutely no right to anyone else's body. The decision to get involved with you is theirs. You have nothing to do with it. She is a person, not your property, and you are not entitled to put your hands on anyone else. It does not matter what she is wearing; her clothes have nothing to do with her decision of whether or not to have sex with anyone. How much she had to drink has only a little bit to do with it, and that is, the more she drinks, the more you should stay the hell away. Don't do it. Just Don't Think About It!

These are things I began to think about in college, but did not clarify themselves until far after I got out of college.

8

THIS ONE TIME... AT
HOCKEY CAMP

THE SUMMER AFTER GRADUATING FROM KENT, 1987, I had the opportunity to spend six weeks at Penn State University working hockey camps. I was the goalie coach, which means I had no specific group of kids to be around all day, but was on the ice for about 7 hours a day coaching the goalies during all of the practices. This was good since I was able to work with all of the goalies in the camp, and was able to work with all of the staff. It also gave me a lot of free time for hours at a time, so there was plenty of time to spend at the outdoor pool, a bit of golfing, and at the bars. I did not need a car, and downtown, where I spent almost every night, was walking distance. There were plenty of bands playing in the bars, and there were always people there, since there were a significant number of students in town for summer classes. There were several bands that I really enjoyed, and I definitely did not want to miss this. The dorms were four empty walls with a roommate and no air conditioning and I would have had a hard time sleeping anyway.

Despite the money being good, this experience gave me a great chance to coach, to learn aspects of coaching from the many head coaches that were working there, as well as making contacts with coaches in the college hockey world. The social scene was also valuable for me to grow, most of the fun was the connections to friends while spending all of this time away from the work space. Along with many other staff members, I was never one to stay in when something may be going on, and I had a hard time sleeping anyway, so I went out. I didn't always drink, only once or twice a week or so, but I enjoyed the nights watching bands or having wings at the bars. I was also able to spend time with these people at the pool, working out in the weight room, running, and playing golf. Not a lot of time to myself, at least in the first year or two of this.

One place I was dying to check out for two straight summers, yet scared to even ask about and avoided in the most deliberate way, was the only gay bar in town. I was intrigued, but not enough to expose myself to anything that would derail all of this fun and camaraderie. On the other hand, as time went along, I did call the place to see if they had any drag shows or a drag scene to speak of. They did not have any drag shows or events, but I did find a time where most of the hockey camp staff was either out of town or busy on a weekend and I was in town by myself to check it out. Although I knew there was no real drag scene in the entire area and that bar, I spoke to people there that gave me info on where to look, which was the classified ad section of the student newspaper. Where was Google when I needed it?

Finding a pay phone and using lots of quarters, I called every number that said anything about being a crossdresser, or spending time with anyone looking for a crossdresser, and most were dead ends. One person I connected with owned a RV/trailer lot about 25 minutes away from campus. He would dress in the office trailer after hours and meet people for hookups, although the hookup part was not advertised. I was so excited to meet with someone that I may have something in common with. I arranged to meet him and drove 25 minutes through the country areas to the RV lot, which was surrounded by forests. When I arrived there were two relatively younger, feminine-presenting guys there to greet me, and then she walked out of the trailer. My first thought was 'dude does NOT look like a lady.' She was in a long dress, big gawky clip on earrings, shoes that looked too tight, and no wig, just his short gray men's haircut. Really, this is it? The first person I actually went to see at their own place, sort of a blind date. I was so incredibly freaking nervous I had to stop my knees from crashing together from all of the shaking, in a place out in the middle of nowhere, with woods surrounding a trailer sales lot. I did not expect to find this person to be over forty years older than I was. I am not sure exactly what I was expecting, but I found this to be very creepy and not the glamorous person with the glamorous life that I dreamt about from inside the vault.

We spoke for about 10-15 minutes or so, comparing notes about how we felt inside, but mostly I found out that she has felt the way she felt for a lifetime, since childhood. She is not in a position to dress full time, and that she just wants to dress, feel good about herself, and once in a while, have sex with younger men. The other two younger guys kind of stood there and smiled the entire time. She asked me if I wanted to walk around and come into the office and sit, relax, and chat. This was starting to feel like I was in a movie, and not a family movie. My internal panic button was engaging beyond my control, and I told them all I had to go, that I had to get back to campus for something I had just remembered, and got the hell out of there.

Looking back at this situation, yes, I judged her. I also judged the two guys that were there. It was years later that I understood that all this sixty-plus year old person was doing was finding a time and a place to be herself. In the late 1980s and early 1990s, she was likely stuck where she was, and I do not know how much she knew about who she was when she was my age at the time, which was my early twenties. Who was I to judge? Cell phones were not even invented yet, let alone the internet with Google. I was trying to figure out who was, and here was someone who has a clue who she is, that I wanted to learn from, and I am judging? If I am judging, everyone is judging people like her (and me). I was not sorry for not going into that trailer because, although I was craving being with someone that was like me, I was frightened. I did not know how this was going to end, but I did not want these kids to force me into something with her. I am glad I went to find out, but this episode made me content to stay in the vault, deep in the vault.

As much as I want to try to be kind to myself for trying to learn and not realizing what I was doing, there is still some guilt inside me for being a bit of an asshole to someone who was trying to help me, upon my own request. This was one of just many learning opportunities that I would go through while I moved forward in my everyday world trying to hide so much and moving through life through the lens of my cis het white male privilege.

9

ON MY OWN

IN MAY 1988 I WAS A COLLEGE GRADUATE AND LIVING ON
my own for five months, I felt a freedom that I had never really
experienced. My girlfriend that I was engaged to in college and I
broke up with over the summer, making me feel truly independent.
I accepted a volunteer coaching position at St. Bonaventure University starting in the fall. I was looking to get into coaching at the
college level, and had met the head coach at the Penn State Hockey
camps that summer, and mentioned he could get me some part
time work as a substitute teacher in the school district where he
worked full time, even his position as head coach was a part-time
head coaching position. I was happy to be able to coach at the
college level so I could use my education degree and everything I
had done up to that point to do whatever it took to get into the
coaching world.

Moving to Olean, NY, a small town in which I knew absolutely
no one, was an exciting experience for a young college graduate.
With this new independence I was able to explore a bit about
myself, finding housing and spending money out of my savings for
a used Chevy Caprice Classic on my own, and finding new friends.

The head coach was more than helpful, getting me on his men's league hockey team, which happened to need a goalie since his roommate was the goalie and coming back from injury. He also showed me to the sports bar of choice, Granny's Verona, a place where I was able to hang out. And we would hang out almost every night. I never was one to sit around the apartment that I shared with the other assistant coach, so I would go to the bar at nights. I took part time jobs delivering pizzas at night and as a substitute teacher by day. I was busy, especially as the district found that I could handle the special education kids, and did a respectable job with the kids that presented behavioral problems. This meant I was doing pretty well financially, at least well enough to pay bills, eat, and have a bit of a social life. I was grateful for the pizza delivery job as it provided an opportunity to drive all over town and learn the area, and eat free food, both of which were beneficial. I gave the pizza job up when I was able to land a part time job as assistant manager of the Olean Recreation Center, the local ice rink. My seven years of Zamboni and rink supervision experience made this a perfect match, and I spent time there since that was the home ice for the Bona hockey team.

Once the routine settled in, I found myself with a little down time, time to think about things. I had a couple of dates with women, but nothing really stuck for long. The coaching was fun and rewarding, having a lot of responsibility and making mean-ingful connections with the players, particularly the goalies, which I really enjoyed.

The job at the rink was great, right in my comfort zone, my happy place. Driving the Zamboni, sharpening skates, meeting people who liked hockey, and being trusted to manage a facility made it a very meaningful and enjoyable part time job. While being involved with socializing with people in an environment of which I had expertise, it became a private place for me at the same time. At night, I closed the building, and the high school kids that worked there were gone for the night, but the girls left their magazines all around the skate rental area. The ones that featured fashion and make up: Glamour, Marie Clare, Vogue, and others. It was nice to be able to look at these in such a way that the girls that were somewhere close to my age had the chance to read.

With no internet in those days, this was not only interesting and refreshing to me since I had no one that I could share any of this information with without being caught. By "caught" I mean being a young, athletic coach starting a coaching career and a teaching career as a substitute teacher in classes that the kids who worked there were in, reading magazines that are clearly published for women and commonly known to be popular with teenage girls. I began to dream of myself in that makeup, and in those clothes, and it brought me back to when I was in the attic with my mothers old clothes, when I felt comfortable and normal. And with these thoughts, the dreaded vault returned to my consciousness. As was the case with anytime these thoughts took over my head, the stress returned, and my need to stay more to myself was omnipresent. I was simply not near as sociable while these thoughts were in my head, and seemed as though I was on the constant lookout for a safe way out to experience being myself.

One possible crack to get out of this entrapment was when I discovered the classified ads in the back of these magazines. Information on fetish clothes and shoes was there and how to purchase them. You could mail order things, or call in to apply a credit card to the purchase. After closing the building, I would make a call to a few of those places in the back of the magazines, particularly Michael Salems, a mail order fetish store. They sold five and six inch high heels in large (read "mens") sizes. Crazy high prices and logistics made purchasing these items impossible, but I could call their 800 number and just talk about the shoes, sizes, colors, height of heels, to learn as much as I possibly could about anything that may end up helping me. Once in a while I would mix it up a bit and ask about some of the clothing I would learn about these items, and it was awesome to talk to someone about this topic. I would make up any reason to tell them that I was calling, and it became difficult to come up with a different story each time. I did the best I could, as this was the only release I had, and the only real chance I had at learning anything about who I was and what I wanted. I did not yet really realize who I was, but I know these conversations occurred from deep within the most foolproof privacy. This was not only my first experience at living on my own while as an adult rather than a student, it was also my first experience to truly explore my life inside the vault. Being by myself and somewhat independent, going different directions and not answering to any one person to actually provide an opportunity to experiment and try to learn what put her in the vault in the first place.

And for those who may be wondering, no, I was not on the clock once I locked the door. I would not dare do anything that would make anyone question my hours, but I was still in the building, safely, where I existed much of the time, secured inside a locked building with an excuse I could easily come up with in case a police officer or a city official came by.

10

THE LOVE OF MY LIFE

ON AN ABSOLUTELY PERFECT, 81 DEGREE SUNNY DAY IN the spring of 1989, after the hockey season was over, I was walking down a street near the dyke next to the river, since I knew there was a small neighborhood park and I wanted to play basketball. I was bouncing a basketball down the street, with steady, rhythmic pounding interrupted by an occasional dip or uneven portion of the sidewalk in one of the oldest neighborhoods on the south side of Olean, NY. I was looking for an alley that would lead to a park that I had heard had an outdoor basketball court, and I could feel myself getting a bit thirsty due to the slight bit of exercise, and from the pollen that was flying in the air, while at the same time, I could not ignore the sweet smells of the freshly blooming flowers and honeysuckle in some of the yards. While looking between each house on my right, all of which were built in front of the Allegheny River over 100 years ago, I happened to glance forward when I saw a friend who also taught at BOCES, Maria, walking down a cross street roughly two houses away on the opposite side of Green Street. With her was a woman who took my breath away. Her friend was with a very thin and attractive girl around our age with a wide, fun smile and huge, high blonde 80's hair. I could barely wait for the two cars to pass before I could cross the street, and as I approached, I was smitten immediately, and Maria introduced us. I became thirstier due to the nerves that shot through me. Then, I mentioned I was looking for a park to play basketball, which was weird for me since I was not a great basketball player. I was just looking for something to do to get a bit of a workout on a beautiful sunny day. She mentioned her family was into basketball, and the three of us stood and talked for a while. I forgot about the park, and was completely immersed in getting to know this goddess that was a Catholic school junior high teacher who lived with her grandmother while her other grandmother lived across the street. I was able to smell a faint stale scent of smoke on Maria, while I was well aware of the sweet, apricot and rose aroma on Marian. I'd never seen pale skin and cut-off sweats look so radiant, she wasn't trying to be beautiful, she just was. The white tank with the red stripe didn't announce her; it revealed her, like sunlight catching the right angle for just a moment. Despite the nerves, I knew I had to leave my shyness behind, I wasn't letting it cost me this chance. I explained what I was up to, why I came to town, and that I had just graduated from Kent State a little over a year ago. She mentioned she just graduated from the University of Vermont a year ago and explained she knew the town since her relatives regularly visited throughout her life and had a rather large extended family in the area. I felt her warmth and calmness as it was omnipresent within her as she listened to me, allowing my words so easy to formulate and glide smoothly out of my mouth. I was excited, yet relaxed, a position I was not always in while meeting a girl I really liked and wanted to get to know. Finding the park and playing basketball did not seem at all important anymore.

As we eventually parted ways, I did not want this impromptu rendezvous to end, probably saying "nice to meet you," or "it was really nice to meet you," five times or more, causing things to be a bit awkward as we finally said goodbye. As we reluctantly turned and walked in opposite directions after our euphoric conversation, I turned around to take one last look at her walking in the other direction and I saw her turning back to do the same. A bit of an awkward moment, but as our eyes connected and we both chuckled in the slight embarrassment of being caught. I turned back around on my way, not daring to look again, despite my desire to do so. I instead saw many of the baby bunny rabbits that were running around playing and grabbing food from the ground while I continued my way to find the park. I knew I had to see her again, and as I mindlessly shot hoops, I knew that this is the girl I want to be with forever.

Years later Marian and I reminisced about the moment and she mentioned that Maria said as they were walking away, "If you want to meet him again, he will be out at Granny's this Friday, and maybe Copperfields (a sports bar and a dance bar, respectively) We can run into him easily." I guess I had a reputation of socializing every chance I had. We saw each other that weekend, and soon saw each other every day from that point forward. I could not get enough of our time together, and it was time to look for a new apartment, so I asked her to move in with me. She was currently living with her Nana, her namesake, and whose house I was at every night helping her grade papers. She was apprehensive since she had a good arrangement and was extremely close with her Nana, and she felt that she would not want to move in unless we were married. I mentioned that I intended for that to happen, however, we did need to get to know each other a bit better first. I was so sure, I could have married her on the spot, although I knew that was not the best idea, and was worried about how people would accept that. She moved in and we were deep in love, getting to know each other's interests. Fifteen months after we met, we were married with a large wedding at the St. Bonaventure Church the summer after that school year on August 18, 1990, and a reception that people still talk about being among the most fun they have been to.

The week after we were married, we went on a four day honeymoon to Montreal, then packed all of our stuff in a Ryder moving truck and moved to Clinton, NY where I took the next step of my young hockey coaching career as the Assistant Men's Hockey Coach at Hamilton College. This coaching odyssey would take us to Kent State, my old stomping grounds and a second home for me, for a three year stint. After three years, the university dropped the program that I played for, helped improve and elevate, and coached as we matriculated into the CCHA, arguably the strongest Division I hockey league in the nation in those years. This not only broke my heart, it pissed me off that they would do such a thing to add women's sports and comply with Title IX regulations, and forced me to find another job. This program meant the world to me and it was unconscionable to me that they had to kill the Men's Gymnastics and Men's Hockey programs just to add women's programs, Women's Soccer and Golf, to fall more in line with Title IX and gender equity. The attitude of the athletic department was to just move on and forget the two sports never existed. At the same time, I did not have a problem with the school adding women's programs, and new opportunities, just not at our expense, or anyone's expense. I was friends with many women athletes at the school and often showed up to watch their games and support them. The fact that my job was dissolved due to something that was out of my control not only affected me, but also Marian, who was in the process of getting her masters degree there free thanks to my employment, which was ending at the end of the year. I did not have good feelings about the University and the University president for a long, long time.

Needing a job, I tried my hand at my first head coaching job with an opportunity in Lakeland, Florida of the Sunshine Hockey League, a very low level professional hockey league at the time. I made a lot of mistakes and learned a lot, however, the franchise was sold after that year and I had an opportunity to coach Junior hockey in Dubuque, IA of the United States Hockey League, the premier junior league in the country, featuring the majority of the top college prospects in the country. This was an incredible opportunity, again learning a lot in a highly competitive environment with some of the best talent in the country. I was there roughly a year and a half when I was fired the weekend before Thanksgiving after a losing start to the season, and we then moved to Ann Arbor, MI so I could work in the Ice Arena business. It was there that Marian and I were able to be together more often, with actual regular working hours. Every move we made, Marian had to give up her teaching or tutoring job, or whatever it was she was doing at the time so I could pursue my dream of a hockey coaching career. With no opportunities available in the middle of a hockey season for a job, we decided the ice arena business was the next best thing, maybe a bit more stable. I began refereeing hockey, and our duplex apartment located 8 doors down from Michigan Stadium provided a lot of excitement on fall afternoons, along with the hockey that is going on in hockey crazy Ann Arbor and the greater Detroit area. It was at this time, after 9 years of marriage and a lifestyle that resembled that of most people we know with daytime work hours and most nights and weekends off, we decided to actively pursue having kids.

11

MY BETTER HALF

NOW THAT I WAS OUT OF SCHOOL AND MARRIED, THE noise from the vault began to shout more loudly after I settled in a new town and adjusted to a new schedule, which was always hectic, working long hours with a lot of responsibility, making it difficult to tend to my other half. Any research for the matters from inside the vault would have to be done after all of my responsibilities are done, in a place where I do not know anyone or that I know none of my players would be, and of course without the knowledge of anyone that knew me by my deadname, which in those days amounted to every person I knew. This meant on recruiting trips, the rare times when Marian would be out of town visiting family during the season when I was not able to join her, or a rare time I would be out at night after coaching, playing or reffing a game and before I came home. All of this time, I still needed to rely on classified ads in the local alternative scene papers, or the Yellow Pages to find places such as gay bars, adult book stores or novelty shops to ask questions about men who dress up as women, men that *want* to dress up as women, and the terminology, personal stories, and every single thing that goes along with it. A lot of this information gathering during these times would be done by the phone to get hours, directions, and descriptions of the business. Once I found a gay bar, it was not very difficult to get information about what was going on in the local scene. When my locations were in larger populated areas it was easier to get lost from anyone that knew me, and get information from strangers that I would likely not see again.

This took a lot of planning and preparation. I made sure not to sacrifice my work time, not only because I wanted to succeed, win, and make the best coaching career that I could, but also I did not want to give anyone I was working with a reason to think I was not doing my job, and more importantly, why I was not doing my job. These opportunities to venture out to explore who I was typically happened late at night in gay bars or adult book stores, which worked out well since most of the mainstream people I knew and worked with were in bed during those hours and did not seem like they would frequent those places. I just had to be sure I was safe and sober, so I would not be in a situation where I could not get out of any potentially dangerous situation that may come up so I could be present for the people, jobs, and activities in my "real" world.

The hockey program was disbanded at Kent State by the university president in 1994 after the third year of coaching there. I was devastated since our program was on the rise that a lot of us players worked hard to develop, and I lost a job I truly loved in a place we loved to live. Despite the feelings of loss and frustration, I returned to Kent State each summer for two or three weeks to work hockey camps, ever since the time I left as an assistant coach of the varsity program when it was shut down, until the year that everything was shut down due to COVID-19, totalling 28 years. The weeks consisted of relatively long days, dealing with younger kids, including my oldest child when she was old enough to play, coaching them on the ice either two or three times per day, but provided the time I needed to be able to explore. I stayed in the dorms with the campers and staff, and was responsible for waking up the campers, and taking them to breakfast each day. I liked the earlier ice times and preferred coaching the younger kids, not only because I enjoyed that age level but also they typically skated a bit later in the morning, and were finished on ice relatively early, in the late afternoon, leaving the evenings free, so it worked out for the best that I worked with the younger groups. We would take them to breakfast, lunch, and usually do some sort of activity when we were not on the ice. As a head coach of the group, I would have to plan the on-ice practices out and give roles to all of the assistant coaches and counselors that were working with us before we went on the ice to coach. After the on-ice responsibilities were finished, I would grab something to eat, then go back to the dorm to maybe have a nap or watch baseball on TV. In my mind all day long, I was trying to figure out what to do at night, usually between going out with the staff, or doing my own thing in Akron about 20 minutes away. Often, the decision was already made on what to do during each evening by the time dinnertime rolled around.

Mondays were the huge nights at the Interbelt Night Club in Akron, a gay dance club that featured drag shows on Monday nights, and I could not get enough of it. The other coaches and camp staff members stayed back in Kent were either in bed, or out socializing somewhere in town. I played it off as if I was planning to go to bed early, that's if anyone bothered to ask what was happening on a Monday night. I would get over there at some point between 10:30 and 11:00pm to avoid paying the cover charge, which was $10 cash. Cash was used exclusively from inside the vault, to not leave a paper trail of any kind. Since they allowed 18 year olds in there, there were a lot of younger kids and there was always a drag show, which was supposed to start at 12:30 am, but always seemed to start 15-25 minutes late. You'd think I'd be tired the next day, but I wasn't, I was invigorated. There was an outdoor patio where people would go out and smoke and talk, and a little shack out there selling hot dogs, pizza, and other little things to eat. I usually enjoyed myself out there since I was never one for dancing, I could not dance a bit, but mostly because we could talk out there without having to yell through the music. I never got into dancing as a kid, with being too "sissy" for a tough little athlete in those days, at least in my own mind. I remember these days in the gay bars mostly for the people I met.

A young, pretty drag queen named Marilyn was a hairdresser from Eastern Ohio who lived as a guy and was active in the LGBTQ scene at the time where she did shows and organized events. Marilyn was attracted to me. I was not sure if I was attracted to her but I was drawn to her lifestyle, and what she was able to do: live as a woman at least a part of the time. She knew I thought I wanted to be her, and dress the way she does. She liked me and preferred me as a dude which I almost always presented as in the early years. We became friends and one that I actually was able to keep in touch with by phone (this was before cell phones). These were long distance calls from landlines at the time so I had to have a story for the call for Marian in case she saw the phone bill. The story was always calling a friend from Kent, which was true.

Marilyn gave me terrific insight into the difference between a drag queen, a transvestite (do not use this word), cross-dresser, and a transsexual (I don't like this word, either). She also talked about tranny chasers, who are the cis guys that are always around trying to get the trans femmes to have sex with them. These types of men are attracted to women that have the same anatomy as themselves. I did not realize that I was considered to be a chaser by some of the gender nonconforming people, and from that point on it was imperative for me to disclose that I was there because I felt like I could be one of them. Although I may like their looks or may be attracted to them, I was not there to pick them up or to have sex. I simply wanted to get to know them as people and learn how they knew who they were, when they knew it, and how they went about becoming who they were in truth. Marilyn was great about that, letting me know so much about what she knew to help me, which inspired me to continue to live in the vault and keep learning about myself rather than turn the lights off in the vault and stagnate. That she and others were willing to share their stories are the inspiration why I'll talk to anyone and listen to them - to pay it forward if you will. Up to this point, I would go into a gay bar dressed as a guy, with my heels in a duffle bag which I might later wear, as long as that bar is not located in an area considered to be in mainstream society. It looked awkward, but it was my way of displaying that I was more of a want-to-be tranny rather than a chaser. An ancillary result was that I was able to experience for a bit what it was like to wear the shoes, and the feeling of vulnerability at the time, without initially realizing it. These feelings were both welcome and exciting. Most importantly, these feelings seemed more natural to me than how I lived my day to day life.

Donald was a drag queen who went by different names depending on her persona she was dressed as, and was very real and down to earth. She was also a hairdresser living in a very stylish old house in an upscale Akron neighborhood. She seemed considerably older than I, was very friendly and not into the drama typically present in the gay scene. We would sit down and talk about her life, and how she managed it. She had her own long hair, which made herself look so natural when dressing to go out to the gay bars. She was such a nice person who just wanted to go down to the bar, be herself, perform once in a while at the smaller shows and have some drinks and talk to friends who were not into playing games. I was thankful for the friendly face and the compassion to help a 'straight guy' who did not have much of a clue who 'he' was.

12

DEAR, DEAR JOHN

THE FIRST PERSON I EVER SOUGHT OUT IN A predominantly normal public environment that I could talk to was during a recruiting trip in Buffalo in 1990. I had checked out of my college-provided hotel and then killed time at a mall on a Sunday afternoon while waiting for a game starting in a few hours. While I was walking down one of the hallways, I, along with everyone else in the mall at the time, saw an obvious crossdresser walking in an over the knee dress, black nylons, 2" black pumps, and an auburn wig. As she walked into Macy's, I mindlessly ignored the typical boundaries of my comfort zone and vulnerability and walked quickly to catch up and meet her, never minding all of the other mall shoppers who stopped and watched her walk across the large hallway, making jokes to their companions. The voice inside my head kept alternating between 1) Don't engage, you may get caught, just watch from a distance, play it safe and 2) Go for it, talk to her, I may never have this opportunity to meet someone like this again. Nervous as hell, to the point I could not think of anything else but, as I approached her at the panty table, I managed to utter, "Hi, how are you? You look really great!"

I am not sure what she said after that, I was so nervous, yet excited and intrigued all at the same time. We spoke for twenty minutes or so, walking around the store as I asked her questions. I was careful to learn as much as I could while tuning out the gawkers, tuning them out the same way I tuned out belligerent opponent fans at games, as I felt this was a once in a lifetime opportunity as I was going through it, and at the same time required a position of vulnerability to do this. I also somehow understood the need to treat her with dignity while realizing this vulnerability, especially among all of the gawkers at the time. It turns out, her son played hockey for a team that I had seen play a few times. The boy's mother usually took him to games, but as his parent, she wanted to be more involved. John was very forthcoming with me, and I disclosed early in the conversation that I feel like I belong doing this, dressing up, and feeling like a woman, but for how long? Just once in a while? Forever? I am not sure how I exactly said that, but she was very helpful in explaining how and why she started this behavior and how she maneuvers through the situation in the present. She made clear that this part of her life led to the end of her marriage. Her situation matriculated to the point where she could not hide it anymore and, at the same time, she had not been out at work. It appeared extremely clear that any chance I had would mean significant loss of so many people in my life. Possibly, all of the people in my life.

She invited me to her house, and with plenty of time on my hands, I accepted. I was anxious to go see what was in her closet, and how she managed two lives. I asked where she got her information on how to navigate this lifestyle, and was told Nugget Magazine. Nugget was a porn magazine that I came to find out was very trans-oriented. The thing I took from her, and I still resonate to this day, was her answer to an uncomfortable question:

"How does it make you feel when everyone stares at you and makes fun of you? Everyone knows you are not a real woman?"

Her response was, "I see women all the time that look like crap. There are women everywhere you look that were born women, and either do not take care of themselves, or are just not pretty. I feel like I am no worse than they are." I thought of how inappropriate that sounded, misogynistic even, what even is a "real" woman? Trans women are women. But I understood her point to be that people can present as they wish. I have never forgotten this reply and it sticks with me 25+ years later as I came out, or even when I was sneaking around, that I belong looking any way I want to look since most of it I could do nothing about, and dress how I want to dress, and be myself was my choice and no one else's. When I get the chance, safely, I will be myself regardless of how others see me. I will add, though, I would try to look as pretty as possible since l believed that life would be easier for me if I do not look out of place, when my look is put together, or when I feel I am not diffi-cult for others to look at. Even though I had no idea that I could ever become the person who is trapped in the vault, my vision of that person would be that of a beautiful trophy wife. While I currently see myself as the happiest when I am dressed well with hair and makeup on point, John's statement, along with her brav-ery, helps me if I have any second thoughts regarding my looks.

John was extremely helpful and it was a very warm visit, until I heard her ask, "Do you want a blow job? If you want a blow job... I'll give you one."

I did not know where that came from; I was not the least bit attracted to John, and did not give any indication I was there for any sexual reasons. I got the feeling that it seemed that it was the way it worked, and the way it was, that it was expected that gender-queer people were fetishized, and were expected to perform sexual favors as if it was their duty, as if it was the price to be paid to have any opportunity to live their authentic lives. It was just how it works. While it put a damper on the encounter, it did not taint the entire experience, as I came out of her apartment and was really enlightened, and it was an impetus for my journey and my early belief that I could actually one day find out who I was. Was this who I was? Was my story, and my future, just like John's?

Not so fast.

13

VALERIE, THE PRIVILEGE OF KNOWING YOU

THE MOST INTERESTING AND TALENTED PERSON I MET at any gay bar was Valerie. Valerie was the first 24-hour woman (the word they used to describe a trans woman in those days) I had ever met and got to know. From the Akron area, a tall, black performer, Valerie was beautiful at 6''4" without heels, and talented beyond belief. She made her own clothes for the shows, which were flawless and sang some of the songs herself, rather than lip sync, which is the usual. If she was at the bar, she was in heels no matter what. She performed at the drag shows at the Interbelt and tended bar on another night of the week at another gay bar. Oh yeah, did I say she was beautiful? She was beautiful, both with makeup and with only her own glowing skin, large piercing brown eyes and her ever present large and engaging smile. Her natural hair was straightened and hung below the shoulders when it was not covered by her many natural looking wigs. She was always the star attraction at the shows, which drew overflow crowds, especially on Monday nights.

Valerie was not just a local icon and a black 24-hour girl in the late-night, queer world of gay bars and street life, but a person, and one that was basically shunned in the real world. A girl this smart and talented could not get a job where she could live as herself during the day. She could not get a job as a cashier, or anything else, for two simple reasons: she was black and she used to be a dude. For a person of this description in the early 1990s, there seemed to be no chance. In the daytime, in the regular, cis-het patriarchal world, the one in which I lived in for pretty much 98% or more of my time, she was in the same category as all of the other black 24-hour girls at the time–unemployable, many of whom were unhoused or housing challenged. And if you were unhoused, there were a number of things that seemed to happen. The most common ways to survive this life was the drug scene, which often included either using and addiction if they were not dealing, and the other was survival sex. Both of these avenues were the likeliest ticket to employment and/or housing for these folks.

I stayed rather far away from both of these avenues. I was not going to get involved with these occupations as a means of survival. It was here that I began to understand the concept of privilege, decades before I really learned about it and that was a more prevalent idea. I understood it to mean that if I would transition into this type of person that has changed genders, then this is the life that awaits me. After going through college and earning a bachelors and a master's degree, and having a job I loved where I can coach hockey for a living, and a wife with whom I was hoping to be a parent, how could I throw all of that away and allow myself to barely even survive? Could I go to the bars and the streets late at night every night? I clearly understood what I would be throwing away during this, but, what if it is who I actually was? I picture myself in the vault with a small superball bouncing around the four walls, ceiling, and floor of that cold concrete vault, and it will not even stop, no matter how quick my reflexes are. All of the traffic inside my head was incredibly annoying and ridiculously complicated, and began to escalate a bit with each opportunity to learn more about myself.

So I have learned and figured out the privilege scale before it became a thing, right? Hell no. Somehow, I neglected to see color. I mean I saw color, I knew these 24-hour girls were lacking respect from the white world, and I was aware of a few black drag queens and other queer people in these places that had difficulty getting jobs, as well. For some of them, it seemed to be a motivation factor, they were getting by and they were living the lives they felt they needed to live, and that was enough. But most others had such a difficult time. What my tunnel vision cut out of the screen, was the fact that these queer black people had such a disadvantage. The main reason was simply that they had black skin, and the people that were hiring were typically white. In one conversation I had with a queer, feminine-presenting black guy, he explained to me that he was interviewing for a job the next day, and his goal was to be a cashier. He had never had a job before, and was really excited. I asked how he felt about his chances, he said, it will probably go just like the others and end before it starts. When I asked if he had any classes or training for interview skills, he snapped back, "How the FUCK do you think I can afford that? Ain't like they taught us that shit in school."

Whoa. A bit of a wakeup call. I am sure I had said it in some condescending way, as if they have to pay attention to those opportunities if they planned on getting a job. He put me into my White Cis-Het Male place. He left to get a drink or something, I felt like a selfish, pompous jerk-off. I was embarrassed. I was still confused and really did not look into this anymore, the vault had more of my attention. I hoped he got the job, but I never saw him again to ask him or to even apologize.

Another time, years later, I was leaving the bar at closing time. I mentioned to the guy working the door, a very large and imposing bald white guy, that there are always so many cops around here at closing time. He said, "Yeah, they think there is going to be trouble here, if not, they will find some."

I asked what that meant, he replied, "They know there will be close to 300 gay black people leaving this place around the same time and they are easy targets." I asked "Who's they?" He said, "The black people. They aren't going to fool with you, they are going to find some of them to screw with. They make a bunch of arrests a night, those fucking assholes! It's bullshit."

That conversation offered insight, but what I did not know is if there was drug trade going on, or if drunk people were going to be behind the wheel. There were plenty of white people drunk, behind the wheel after ingesting illegal things, but somehow I figured the cops were doing their job. I look back at that conversation a great deal differently today, and I look at it with some guilt in my heart.

Back to Valerie. I learned a lot from her, and one time I picked her up to have coffee in the morning, away from the late night scene. She looked great without makeup and definitely passed as a woman, and was a nice, humble person. She was afraid that if her partner would find out she was out with a cis-het guy he would not be happy, especially if her partner was trippin.' Of course, she didn't mention that until we were at the coffee shop. We were not after each other sexually or romantically, although there was definitely something there between us that made us a bit more than just acquaintances becoming friends. I knew at that point in time I was not ready for her world. Honestly the coffee shop was out of the way, one where no one I knew would ever go. Not taking any chances even then, on brand, I checked every single person in the place to make sure no one would know me. I was impressed at her vision and enjoyed our conversation about how that community was going to be a lot safer with changes that were wishfully coming from the democratic controlled state government at the time. I remember her saying that "it will probably not happen in my lifetime."

Wait a second, Brianne, you are not ready for her world? WTF?

Honestly, I knew what world I lived in, the one where my education and work ethic was earning me positions in the coaching world, in a career that I hoped would lead me to a head coaching job. To be caught with a black transvestite (the name used at the time, and how trans people were described in my world in those days, primarily as a derogatory descriptor. It is taboo now– don't use this word!) could be the end of not only that dream career, but the end of my marriage. I realized that I had put myself in these positions, and positions that I thought I needed to be ashamed of in my "real life." In short, I was ashamed of myself, but did not know how to admit that or deal with thinking my "real life" had any more value than the life that had this woman in it. I felt like a complete asshole, like I was completely twisted up in the corner of the vault. This icon, who was risking her safety by having coffee with me and helping me discover myself so I could someday just dance out of this constricting vault, was someone I dreamed I could follow in the footsteps of and be comfortable within myself, with no concrete walls and steel door of the vault. That I judged her to be in another social situation and knowing that I wanted to be like her but was too scared to do so simply because of the privileges of being cis het, and most importantly, white. I have since felt a lot of guilt despite the immense power of the learning experience.

After about an hour of conversation at the diner, I dropped her off at her house and hugged goodbye.

The following summer, while back in town for camp, I showed up at the same bar, the Interbelt, on a Monday night with a huge crowd expected, and looked around and saw several pictures of Valerie on the walls. I had to ask what these were there for, the doorman muttered in a soft tone, "Valerie died, tonight is a tribute to her." What were the chances I would be back in town for this?

"WHAT!? OH MY GOD, HOW???" I yelled.

"She was murdered, shot." One of them sternly said. "Murdered." I asked if they knew who did it, and why, they really did not know for sure what happened, but they seemed to think it had to do with a jealous person who she lived with, or someone who did not want to be caught with a girl "like her." There were rumors going around that they arrested someone, but no one had details. Her many friends at the bar had a hard time finding out, since according to the police report, a black male with her dead name was mentioned in the paper, not Valerie, and that was the end of it, no details up to that point of the investigation.

So the last time I had seen Valerie was months ago, when I was trying to be a friend and hide the entire thing at the same time. She was not even listed as a trans person in the paper. This crap still goes on today. In 2020, 37 trans people were murdered because they were trans, more than any year that has been reported. Some of these victims are dead named by either the police, or their parents, so the names are unrecognizable when it is printed in the newspaper. It is widely believed that many more are murdered but are not identified as trans, despite the ever increasing advocates that track these statistics. Valerie was among the best of us, she did not deserve to be killed. In death, she deserved the dignity of being called Valerie, which is who she was. On November 20, 2020, I took the opportunity to memorialize her at the candlelight vigil in Schenectady. Rest In Power, Valerie, I think of you often, and I am proud of you more than you could have ever known.

Back to the privilege thing. It was a couple of decades later that I realized that I was a complete asshole for going for coffee in public with her, but being ashamed of it, and going to all the lengths to assure that I will not be discovered with this person. As much as I was trying to reach out, I was doing just as much to keep her in her world, and not to 'elevate' her into mine. I was terrified that I realized I would have a lot of explaining to do, and I was not willing to risk my privilege, my job, wife, and "credibility" to go through this. Although the vault created the barrier for this behavior, this guilt still haunts me at times, and is at the top of my mind while advocating and living as a member of an underrepresented community.

I learned so much from you, Valerie. You and so many others deserved so much better, from me and from our society.

14

ZEBRA TOUGH

I HAVE OFFICIATED SPORTS FOR ALMOST HALF OF MY years, in both of the sports I love the most, baseball/softball and hockey. In the spring of 1980, my freshman year of high school, I took the umpire class and became a baseball umpire as soon as I was eligible. Although it was nerve-racking at times, I enjoyed myself, and locked into my attempt to be a competent, consistent umpire. I did a good job as a first year umpire and was promoted to higher level games during that first year, progressing each year through high school.

The one thing they tell umpires is that you have to have thick skin because someone is going to question every call. You have to make a decision on every play, and you have to be able to sell your call. At the same time, you need to stand your ground, and do not allow coaches, players, or fans to influence you or intimidate you. The senior umpires would work with us younger ones with how much chirping or arguing to take before you warn them and eventually throw the person out of the game. The biggest thing is to have the confidence to make your call and stand by it. What I actually saw could be interpreted as arrogance, and it was a difficult message to learn. What it all boils down to is that you have to be tough. Coaches and players, as they get older will try to work umpires, even if you have the best, most accurate strike zone, hustle all over the field, and know the rule book cold, if you are not tough enough to take the bitching, yelling, and screaming, you will fail to earn the respect to control a game.

I really enjoyed umpiring baseball and softball games. I loved the idea of being in charge, and I used my loud voice to my advantage, when calling balls and strikes, and letting people know what was going on. I craved control that the games demanded, and it did give me great experience dealing with adults, a lot like my other job at the rink did. I worked in a couple of divisions where I had developed the reputation that I would call strikes using a relatively large strike zone, and was consistent with calling the corners. It was a way to earn respect, and was a great learning experience for me that you can earn respect through hard work. It was a fun way to make money during the summer, and since our association always had tournaments during the Memorial Day and Fourth of July weekends, I did not have to go on any family outing to the country, which I wanted no part of. My best gig was when I was asked to call senior women's softball games, made up of college women, and an excellent level of ball. I worked those games alone, and made $50 per game. It was an amazing gig for a high school kid, especially in those days.

This situation was intimidating at first as I was amazed at the speed of the game and how talented the players were, just an incredible skill level. Secondary to this, they were girls, and they were a lot older than me. It was difficult for me to speak to them the way I did the other divisions that I worked, but I simply treated them as I would an adult, and stuck to my job, tried my best to stay professional. The coach of the one team was our athletic trainer for my Junior Hockey team, so I was not necessarily thrown to the wolves, but the first few games were nerve racking.

A random person asked, "Was there a difference between the male athletes and the female athletes?"

My response was, "Not much, really, the way they played the game was every bit as intense as the men. The difference is how they were treated."

How women are perceived and treated is different from the way men are perceived and treated, and thus, are treated differently by umpires. A perfect example, one that we all have heard a version of, is when I was working a game with our Umpire in Chief, a man very dedicated to the craft of umpiring. I was working a game with him at the Senior Women's Division in a tournament, after I had been working games for only a couple of years. Again, these girls were much older than I was, and a girl argued an out call I made on a tag play. It was one of those plays where it was difficult to see, and I may have missed it, but decided to sell it and stand my ground since I did not know for sure. I did know that I had to take some grief on it, she probably had a point. It ended the inning, so I asked my partner what he thought, he came back with, "Let me tell you something about umpiring girls. They are whiney, they are bitchy, they are complainers, they complain about everything. You will not win, they are always right, and you cannot talk sense into them, so don't let that bother you."

It bothered me. Although it was the best I could do at the split second, I felt the player may have had a point. I was emotional because of this scenario so his words actually talked me down from the ledge and I felt better about this incident. This came from an experienced umpire, and the umpire that was in charge of all of us, someone all of us looked up to, so he must know what he is talking about. So in my analysis of the situation, as a young man, what he said meant something. He must be right, and I honestly took this advice with me for a couple of decades. It was a long time before I realized that life was much different than that; that they did not bitch and complain any more than the guys do. When guys argue it means men are tough and will not back down, when it comes from women it's "bitching and complaining and holding grudges." There are plenty of examples where this gender role inequality manifests itself, but this was spelled out to me in a way that I could not have learned on my own any other way than this apparently real-life situation. This was reinforced often in every situation and with any group of men I interacted with, and just another in a large collection of reasons that I could not just outrightly advocate for women, thus I was scared the dudes would wonder why I was defending them, and I wanted to stay far away from that line. These gender roles and stereotypes pushed me deeper into the vault.

Decades later, this had me thinking about transitioning in uncomfortable ways: Did I really want to venture into this world and give up this privilege of being respected just for my male gender? The idea is challenging–coming out would mean the loss of friends, harassment, physical and mental abuse, and likely worse if I did decide to address my gender conflict. Add to that this example, which spells out a general level of disrespect towards women and makes a solid case that I should not consider addressing the conflict I was having about my gender identity, but something else going on inside the vault and this became quite confusing to me.

Fast forward to fifteen years later, I moved to Ann Arbor, Michigan in 1997, after two years of coaching Junior Hockey in Dubuque, Iowa, where the players were boys between 18 and 21 years old. We had a losing record to start the season and by Thanksgiving I was fired. After ten years of coaching, I had the opportunity to work for a company in the ice arena business. It was great to learn the business side of the rink, and I was busy a lot of time, just like when I was coaching for a living. I missed being involved with the game a lot, but I did not quite miss coaching that much. With hockey so popular in Michigan, and especially the greater Detroit area, there always seemed to be a need for officials, so I decided to scratch the hockey itch with being a referee. I enjoyed this very much as it gave me a chance to learn the game from a different perspective, and make good money doing it. I also played hockey on a men's league team, but I really enjoyed learning things from the referee side of things.

Of course, officiating hockey is another one of those activities where you put up with verbal abuse, and the need to display confidence and a tough exterior is paramount. You do need to be diplomatic and respectful to the players and the coaches, but in youth hockey, the only two people on the ice that are getting paid are the referees, so everyone else feels they have the right to shout what they feel they need to address at the referees. It is important to be decisive and be able to handle some abuse, and that is what is taught and is driven into you. This drive was a strong part of the hockey officiating culture, before the youth hockey's national governing body stepped in to install rules governing the behavior of coaches, players, and spectators, which would not come before another ten years or so. All we had back then was our knowledge of the rule book, our own conviction to sell the calls we make, and the hope that the leagues step in to supplement any discipline that was needed.

In the sport of hockey, officials dealt with a lot of complaining from coaches and players in youth hockey, but also from the players in the men's adult leagues. Many of these players see the players and coaches on television barking at officials, particularly on the way to the penalty box, and figure it is their right as well. It is critical that you display decisiveness in your calls, not show that it bothers you and that you will only take so much before you give another penalty for unsportsmanlike conduct or toss them from the game. The threshold of how much you need to take has lowered a lot since those days, but the bitching by the players and coaches to the point of being penalized is still there.

This is definitely not an environment for a person to be considered soft or weak, actually it is just the opposite. Some coaches and men's league players do try to gain an advantage on the referee, some by intimidation, where they bark at every call, hoping to get the referee to go along with them. Some just like to scream and yell, they do it to their players and officials alike. The key is not to give in to them. The majority of men's league players enjoy the game, want to be safe, and have a good time while trying to win the game. Others, within the minority, but they are there none-theless, try to establish their superiority over the opponents, with dirty play that is not only against the rules, but dangerous. A good number of calls could go either way in a hockey game, and players are always trying to gain an advantage. For me, I have always had a problem with the player who waits around while no one is looking, including often the opponent, and does something like trip them, slash them with the stick, punch in the head, or something dirty. I always try to catch that behavior and penalize it, and try to be consistent with it. They do it to take out their frustrations for a penalty that was not called against that player, or they are just frus-trated for some reason or the guy just plays like that and is a jerk. Whichever the case, it is vital that the official has their emotions under control but also does not allow the irate player to take advantage of them. It is no place to be soft and weak, and it is a difficult road for those that are considered soft and weak.

Perhaps the largest show of masculinity is in the official's locker room, where the theme is "boys will be boys," and the jokes – often rude and crude – are always flying. Usually these are very small spaces, with one shower and space for two to four people to get dressed and ready for the game. Officials do get naked briefly to change into gear or to go in and out of the shower, just as the players do, and it puts someone who questions their gender in a weird position. If you go into another room to change, it could be taken that you are a little weird, because men, particularly hockey players, are used to the locker room and most of us referees are former players. That room is typically a place where boys can be boys, with all of the sexist and homophobic jokes and teasing that goes along with it. The official is often only with one other person, usually a person with the same mindset as the rest--to be the one to not take any crap from anyone.

I was friends with many of my officiating colleagues, thus never was I going to do anything to open the vault up even a little bit, not even the turn of one of the many dials. The hockey world is small. Many of us referees know each other as well as many of the coaches and players, and the grapevine spreads out far and fast. Ain't happening. Not in a rink where I work, and practically live and love to spend my time. Never. Although there were a few women officials, the official's room was another one of those places where I was playing the part of a tough person, who laughed at the occasional sexist joke while trying to fit in the man's world, not feeling comfortable the entire time.

15

WHERE WERE YOU WHEN I REALLY NEEDED YOU?

BY THE TIME THAT I WAS LIVING IN THE TWENTY-FIRST century, I was trying to catch up to social media. Well, sort of. Around 2010 or so, I joined Facebook. The Mustangs, the adult women's hockey team that I have been coaching at the rink since 2005, convinced me to get on Facebook. So I did. I posted a couple of things, did not know how to post a picture, but pecked my way through it with the help of a friend, and kind of left it at that. A couple of years later, Marian took an interest in our relatives and friends' stories and took over the account. She began posting family pictures, stories, and enjoyed finding former classmates and other friends to stay in touch with. Since my name was on it, some of my former teammates, players that I had coached and other old friends jumped on as well, and I sort of lived that experience through Marian's management of my Facebook account.

Now around 2014 or so, I discovered Twitter. I was still not all that keen about posting, since I really was intimidated about almost anything online, and not anxious to get into fights with strangers. I started paying attention to a few topics, in no partic-ular order: St. Louis Cardinals baseball and sports writers, political commentators, and trans twitter. The baseball topic served me well as my escape, the political tweets and commentary woke me up to what is going on in the world, with a person who is a racist, homophobe, transphobe, misogynist and rapist trying to be president. I was locked in, and wanted to learn as much about politics as I could. However, these twitter areas alone did not fulfill my needs.

Trans twitter was the primary reason for my interest in my Twitter account. I followed anyone I could who identified as trans, and with the emergence of Caitlyn Jenner and her popularity, things were really starting to stir in our society, not to mention inside the vault. The climate was beginning to get warm and suffocating in there and being able to read comments, stories, and more from real life trans women made the air stir a little bit inside that vault of mine. I realized that if this is who I am, I am definitely not alone. I must not be all *that* weird. I also realized that trans people come from all walks of life, including writers, actors, IT specialists, college professors, construction workers, bartenders, waiters, former military personnel, truck drivers, and many, many more. The common thread among the trans people who are out that I followed on Twitter, whether they were successfully out or a crossdresser part time, was that they all seemed to have experienced hate and some sort of loss, yet at the same time were free to live their true lives. They would share that the process of coming out became a huge dilemma, while it is the most important and invigorating thing they would ever do, and at the same time, the most devastating event that could have happened. A lot of people would vent about their life situations, the disowning by loved ones, the physical and verbal abuse at work, the loss of employment, and many other unfortunate calamities. The hardship that resonated with me the most were the reactions of spouses, parents, and most importantly, their kids. All of them went through at least some sort of doubt, apprehension or worse from their family members, friends, and colleagues. Before working things out and having people coming around in order for the trans person to be even a bit comfortable in their lives or part of their lives, these people went through a lot of hell before any of this euphoria could be present in their daily lives.

Often on Twitter, I would find various threads to lead me to other articles, trans figures and other content. Once, I found a link to a six-episode drama series called *Her Story*, about two trans-gender women and their struggles with dating, friendship, and their professional lives. It is the first show that I had ever seen where trans people are depicted as real human beings, not an outlier in society that people made fun of, or a trope. To see what trans women really went through on a daily basis was riveting, and made me hungry to learn more. I immediately followed both of the trans actresses in the show on Twitter, and was intrigued that I may be able to buy into the notion that trans people can live normal lives. I needed more, I could really begin to hear the world outside of this vault I had been so locked in here for my entire life.

Another life changing link I clicked on led me to a New York Times Op-Ed piece by Jennifer Finney Boylan, who transitioned into a woman while teaching English at Colby College in Maine. This too was invigorating–a professor at a small, elite academic institution in the Northeastern United States. It seemed strangely familiar, since I work at a small, elite academic institution in the Northeastern United States. I read the piece three times, and that very day, I went out and bought her book, *She's Not There, A Life In Two Genders*. I am a slow reader, and I could not put this book down, and I just had to finish it as fast as I could. She had a wife and two kids, and felt different her entire life, which I found eerily familiar. I finished the book and emailed her right away, just to tell her that I feel like her, that I loved her story, and thanked her for putting the book out there. I remember that I specifically wrote 'I feel like you,' and remember it vividly because I re-read it before I pressed send, and it was the first time I wrote anything like that, and it felt a bit like I was putting myself out there, even though this is someone who has no idea who I am. I just hoped that maybe someday, I could figure it out like she did, and live a comfortable, free life. Still a lot of work to do on my end, but I was willing to continue to figure my way out of that godforsaken vault.

I had read this book in the privacy of my vault. I did not want to be caught reading a book about this subject matter, since it would lead to an automatic outing to my family. Everyone would know that I would not be wasting time reading about an English professor, especially one that turned themself into a girl. So I found time on my own, often at night when everyone else was sleeping. This was difficult, but no different than hiding my clothes, shoes, and everything else.

The next book I dived into was written by another person I followed on Twitter, Janet Mock. Janet is beautiful, centered in the entertainment sphere, mainly focusing on writing, directing, and producing movies and television shows. She is incredibly accomplished and well spoken and her tweets made so much sense to me. The way I resonated with her twitter content inspired me to read her book, *Redefining Realness*. Mock recounts growing up and figuring herself out at an earlier age, and how she was able to come out despite many obstacles, transition, and succeed. I was really starting to feel like these women, as if we had something in common, because we did. The way they described their feelings, the good times, the frightening times, and everything in between had me hooked to her book. Janet has since gone on to write and direct for the TV show Pose, a show about the ballroom scene in New York in the 1970s as the HIV/AIDS epidemic was catching fire in the gay communities all over the country. It tells about the lifestyle of black trans women, many of them thrown out of their homes, and were living in the streets of New York City. The younger trans people would merge themselves into a family that lived in a house managed by a mother, who was often trans. The mothers would look out for them, provide a place for them to live, and assist in their growth to make it on their own. It showed many of their struggles, how they coped and survived, or didn't survive. I watched the show many years later, but I was amazed at Janet. She is such a talent, and a hero of mine.

The time I had a chance to see someone live was May 25, 2015, when Laverne Cox was speaking on campus at Union. I could not believe it, a student group had Laverne Cox, THE LAVERNE COX, come to speak on our campus. She is both an icon and an idol of mine. A tall, beautiful black trans woman, Laverne Freaking Cox was very outspoken on Twitter, and a favorite of mine, and ON OUR CAMPUS! She was gaining fame for her role in Orange Is The New Black, a show about a women's prison, where she played a trans woman cosmetologist in prison. We did not get Netflix at the time, so I did not see her in the show by that point; based on the media coverage, it was clear she would not be insignificant, that she would succeed and make it possible for an entire generation of trans women to flourish. Laverne's presence is powerful; every time the spotlight is on her, she commands the room. The way she spoke her truth for the entire community was unbelievable and I just had to see her.

So on the Sunday of Memorial Day weekend that year, with nice weather, I decided to go see her speak. I did not usually have to work on Sundays at that time of the year. Although this 3:00 pm event in the Memorial Chapel on campus was not something I needed to be at, I could not miss this chance. I told Marian I had to go to campus and check in on the basketball tournament that was renting out our gyms, and rode my bike the one mile to campus. That mile felt like it took a century. I checked in on the basketball tournament right away, which our guys had under control. This left me free to attend the event or to return home.

At around 2:30 pm, a half-hour before the event, I was getting chills, chills of being frightened. I desperately wanted to go to this, had no idea how well attended it would be, but there was a huge problem. I was scared because I was not out; I was still in this goddamn vault. What if I go inside the venue and someone that knows me sees me there? I was positive they would question why that old white man from athletics was attending a black trans woman's talk? They would. I may know some of the faculty moderators, and I know all of the campus safety officers, some who would definitely be there. What would I say if they asked, "Hey, what are you doing here?" I could not come up with an answer in the event they asked that question. Why would I, as everyone knew me, be there on a sunny Sunday afternoon if I was not interested in the speaker. How could I even explain my interest without outing myself? On the flip side, how badly would I kick myself in the ass if I missed this chance? I knew that answer, and I would hate myself for passing up this opportunity. This pressure inside the vault escalated for the entire half hour, and well beyond. Maybe I could sneak in fashionably late? Maybe they would not see me? Maybe the venue would be packed, and it would definitely be hot, and people would wonder what the hell I was doing there, maybe there would be a small crowd so I could just slither in the back and take things in unnoticed. And on and on with these thoughts. I drove myself crazier with each passing minute.

Final verdict: I rode my bike over there, scared to death with every rotation of the pedals, with these questions cycling through my head. When I arrived, I still had not settled it. I parked my bike, snuck up the steps, and after taking about a minute and a half, cracked the door of the Memorial Chapel open to see if I could see anything. The archaic building was packed and boiling hot with no air conditioning. A couple of students in the back turned to see who was entering the sweat box and contributing more body heat to the already unbearable building. At that moment I decided I did not want the slightest bit of attention on me, and holding my breath, I carefully closed the door to make sure there was no sound, backed out and got down the stairs as fast as I could before I could exhale.

The second I reached the sidewalk, I was immediately pissed at myself, pissed that I had no idea how to get out of this goddamn vault, and I was so pissed that I did not have the guts to go in and see a literal trans icon. I had to figure this out, and freaking soon. I am pissing away a chance of a lifetime to see this celebrity because I am chickenshit! I told myself I had to get a look at her. So I walked up to the side of the building, and looked through the open windows, and had a chance to see her; she was absolutely radiant and stunning, larger than life itself. Getting to see her helped decrease some of the pressure within the vault. I felt a little better riding home with the vision of her in my brain, but was still pissed at myself for not going through with the experience of seeing this beautiful, outspoken hero. I made my mind up right then and there that if or when I came out, I would never be a chickenshit, I would be a badass. I would not waste the opportunity to say what I need to say, to talk to whoever I want to talk to, to help whoever needs my help, and do what I need to do, because this could not go on. Something somewhere has got to give, I cannot continue to beat my head against the thick concrete walls of this freaking vault anymore, it is really starting to hurt, in a lot of different ways. I will be confident and not care who sees me in every situation as if it is perfectly normal. I made up my mind I need to own this, and I fucking meant it!

16

LEGITIMATE LADIES LOOKING FOR LIVE JAZZ?

ONE NIGHT, WHILE AT KENT DURING THE SUMMER OF 2016, I no sooner walked into The Square, a small gay bar on Market Street in Akron, Ohio, when Samantha greeted me as I walked outside to the back patio. The friendly trans woman complimented my shoes and began to talk about my outfit. We immediately started to ask each other many questions about our respective journeys, and quickly became friends, which we remain. Samantha is 6'5" with shoulder length wavy hair, wears a size 15 women's shoe, and was still in the coming out process having just started Hormone Replacement Therapy, in which her male hormone, testosterone was suppressed, and she would take estrogen, the female hormone. She worked at her brother-in-law's screen printing shop, and worked long hours for little pay. Samantha loves to sing karaoke and was there with her friend Natalie, a trans woman who is also a talented singer/musician/songwriter. I would meet Samantha a couple times on a Sunday night at the straight bar where Natalie would host karaoke once a week in Akron. Natalie, a very confident, attractive, and self assured trans woman also played piano at another bar, a straight bar, on another night of the week and is also part of a queer band and has recorded albums.

Yes, I had been dabbling into dressing up to go out to the gay bars, or the coffee shops, places that are safe spaces. Once in a while, I would dress up and walk through a mall, then make my escape, before I could talk to anyone, or before anyone who would gawk at me or would mess with me. From there, I would keep taking baby steps as part of coming out. Every one of these steps built on my confidence, enabling me to take it one step further, which could include trying on new clothes and styles, and at times the conversation with the sales girl would turn to my journey. This is what I was using as a mental health tool, as a substitute for a therapist. These encounters gave me the ability to say how I feel about who I am out loud to another human being, someone that does not know me. I was good about reading the room, I did not want to take up their time or chat it up with someone that had no interest. Yet, at the same time, some of these people were sympathetic and admired what I was doing to find myself, and I made friends with some of these sales girls, and are still friends to this day. This meant a lot that someone would take an interest in me and my comfort level, and were very committed to my well-being and my need to look good. This was also great for me to be able to make friends in general, to care about them as much as they care about me. This was both unexpected and invigorating, since I was not good at making and keeping friends in my 'real' life, other than my few really close ones. It turned out to be the best case scenario short of getting actual therapy.

So why didn't I just go find therapy? I could not look into it for fear of getting caught. Even though insurance would cover it, it would generate paperwork, mail correspondence, and a new set of questions from my wife that I would have to answer. I felt the way to go was to stay under the radar as much as possible and utilize my safe space outlets that I am carving out for myself.

The most liberating feeling that ever happened to me to that point was when Samantha and I went to Blu-Jazz, a fancy Jazz club on Market Street in downtown Akron. We went for the first time on a Thursday during an open mic for jazz musicians, and best of all, there was no cover charge. Even better, it had a great atmosphere, accepting staff, and had the downstairs look of a modern day speakeasy. The live music was beyond intoxicating in the dark club, and this is what I think of when I realize why I love jazz music. And most of all, no one we knew in our real lives ever went there, allowing us to be ourselves. Just ourselves.

This was my first time going out truly as Brianne, along with Samantha, dressed up and out in the "mainstream" as ourselves. We literally were treated as ladies, used the women's bathroom, and felt relaxed and invigorated the entire time. The manager approached our table and asked, "How is everything for you ladies tonight? Are you enjoying yourselves?" We conversed for a while, and felt totally validated over this opening question, a question I had never heard addressed to me. Our server was chatting with us as if we were just three girls together out on the town, nothing abnormal about it at all. I remember the feeling of genuine euphoria, and we were totally giddy after two and a half to three hours. When we walked out of that place at the very end of the night, among the last to do so, we could not contain our excitement. I look back and I realized we did not in any way pass, but did not feel judged by anyone in the room and felt amazing that it did not in any way deter them from treating us with respect and validation.

You may be wondering when I changed. Did I leave the dorm dressed? Did I stop somewhere? The answer is no, and I cannot remember being more excited for an event before. I made sure I shaved really well, that I had all of the clothes I would need: a sleeveless peach colored dress that I had bought the previous day at Plato's Closet, a thrift store. I had my favorite 3-inch high heeled sandals, with two clear straps, along with whatever I had for make up. My lipstick was a relatively new creamy dark red that I had found in a parking lot a couple of years prior, and some foundation I believe I picked out of the trash once Marian was done with it without really realizing if it had matched my skin color or not.

From the time I was in the shower around 7:30pm, shaving and gathering my things, I was very upbeat, and all I could see in my mind was myself in these clothes and sashaying into the club with my friend, and all eyes turning on me in affirmation. I had been sure to have my bra already, a non padded D cup underneath my navy blue size XL t-shirt so no one would detect it on my way in or out. Each step down the hall and stairs felt like shedding an old skin, I was leaving as someone new, and it was exhilarating. I felt it, the rush of knowing I was no longer the same person who walked in earlier that day. I could feel the bra latched somewhat tightly around my chest, keeping me aware that it was there and that I was not quite the person any of them thought I was. I had nerves running all the way down my legs making them numb. I felt vulnerable, yet in complete control the entire time, each step gaining more and more confident in the adventure I was about to embark on. Once in the car, I knew I had to be dressed when I arrived, and I knew I had to do some severe double-tasking-driving, undressing and dressing at the same time. I waited until I was at a stop light where there was no other car around, and that did not quite happen. So I decided to take off my t-shirt while driving on I-76 into Akron. Taking the oversized t-shirt off was fine, leaving with me driving around dusk with a somewhat dingy white bra. I was careful to keep my knee and at least one hand on the steering wheel while I was twisting and coiling my peach dress up so I could get it over my head quickly and still see the highway. I was able to get each arm through their respective openings, quickly so it looked to other drivers that I already had this dress on. I left my athletic shorts underneath my dress. My next step was to take my handmade fake boobies, which I made earlier that night in my room with rice filled into the bottom of a thick, sturdy nylon, tied very carefully at the top. A young drag queen gave me this tip about two years prior and I was finally able to try it out! Placing these into my bra gave me the feeling that I was carrying something on my chest, that that may be what it is like to have real boobs. This may be the most euphoric portion of the night, second to the soft material of the dress on my skin. All of my senses, except for maybe my sight on the road was centered on my boobs. This feeling was one that I had never experienced before, but I wanted to have forever. To glance down and see my dress protrude out at the chest was something I never really knew that I wanted, let alone anything I ever thought I could have. In my vulnerability at that very moment, knowing anyone could see me, I felt strongly that I had power in the situation, yet I did not know what type of power. I just felt in charge. Alive. Myself. Nothing the rest of the night would stop me from the ultimate experience of my life.

When I arrived in the parking garage, I felt some serious nerves, anxiety, but those were overtaken by excitement and wonder about how we would be accepted. We had decided on this place based on meeting some of the workers at the bar, so I was looking forward to seeing at least a familiar face. I texted Samantha to see where she was before I applied my foundation. Just small dabs, not wanting to draw a lot of attention to any possible makeup mishaps. Applying lipstick was more of an art project, and it seemed to be the longest 25 seconds that I had spent in a long time. I had experimented with lipstick in the past, and it always made me feel as though I was entering a beauty pageant. It was just the touch to make me feel as though I was someone else, that my dream had somehow come true, all of the imagery, the dreams, the millions of conversations within the confines of the vault were coming out for the ultimate trial, and I was determined to absolutely shine, the spotlight would be on me and my heart was just about to explode out of my chest in anticipation.

I entered the car (not exactly the phone booth) as Clark Kent, and while driving, changed into my hero, Superman, by the time I arrived at the parking garage where I met Samantha. Or did I turn into Lois Lane? Or was it a little bit of both? The entire thing was confusing, but I believe I actually arrived at my destination: I was who I was supposed to be. Myself. Brianne. There was a definite change in how I felt, and how I realized who I was. It was amazing. I felt myself savoring every single minute of it.

Samantha and I met, hugged, told each other how beautiful the other one looked, and how proud we were of each other and ourselves. We knew we were embarking on an adventure that would catapult us into an entirely different life than the ones we were living. I was happy to enter into this new life with my new friend, someone that is going through the same thing that I was. I felt every single step as we nervously walked down the two flights of the musty smelling concrete staircase, feeling the movement of my boobies, which were supposed to produce some sort of move-ment, the balls of my feet feeling each and every step down in my three inch stilettos, and my legs were feeling light and ready to walk into our seats, not even knowing the set up and how many people were actually there. As we entered from the staircase into what we immediately realized was a modern day speakeasy. We approached the front counter, the man and the woman that were the hosts greeted us warmly, making us immediately feel welcome. Tonight was free admission, as it was open mic night, so it was a great night to not spend as much money; the wine we ordered was going to be expensive enough. We were guided in the main room with an elevated stage in the corner to the left, with several musi-cians on stage loudly playing jazz music. The tunes were upbeat yet relaxing, and my mouth became dry as we walked our way through the crowd from the front of the very large room filled with occupied tables. We followed her to our little table midway along a long wall of small tables, for couples to be sitting next to one another on the bench that went along the length of the wall. Once we were seated, I was craving water and a wine menu to satiate my dry mouth that resulted in this exhilarating and somewhat scary experience of feeling the spotlight as two trans girls walking through the middle of the large crowd. One of the girls who invited us saw us and enthusiastically darted over to hug us and talk to us, and told us how beautiful she thought we were, but did not make a huge thing about us being any different. If anyone overheard our conversation, they would think that we are on a normal activity and made us any anyone else feel like we legitimately belonged. She sent the manager over, who we also met at the gay bar a few days prior, and he was extremely welcoming as well. We made small talk with a couple sitting next to us on each side, and I felt like I could talk to anyone that night. And I did talk to as many people as I could that night. Most of the people replied when I asked them something or complimented them on what they were wearing. When I asked the manager where the restroom was, he made sure to reply "the women's restroom is back around the corner to the right."

Going into a women's public restroom for the first time to actually use it was such a rush. I was wary if someone would see me in there and tell me to get the hell out of there, but somehow, I felt that I should be in this bathroom, and could not believe I had not been able to use a women's room before. I felt such a warm feeling as I was walking back to my table and could not wait to tell Samantha about it. She then went right away.

We stayed here until the night was over, around 12:30 am, which had us there for a good two and a half hours. We were still enjoying this amazing night and wanted to savor as much as we could as we waited for most of the people to leave before we climbed the stairs back to the top of the parking garage. We stayed in the parking lot for around 30-45 minutes talking about each portion of this night, from conversations, to going to the bathroom, to how amazing we both felt and that we could not believe that this just happened. I knew this experience would lead to bigger and more exciting things.

This feeling that I had was that in a strange way, I felt normal. Normal in a sense that even though I had never before been in a real situation in this persona, I had a peaceful feeling that this is the way I should look, act, present; that this is the way I am supposed to be. As emotionally high as I felt after this was over, I felt that much more devastated when it came time to drive back to campus and change clothes while driving - again. I had done this countless times before, but this time I was almost defiant, came close to staying in my dress, and coming out right then and there if anyone happened to see me walking into the dorm at 2:35am in the morning. I was actually pissed off when I had to take my shoes off at a stop light, and when I was looking for the cheap makeup remover wipes I had bought about a year ago, hoping with every fiber in my being that they would work to remove my foundation. I then thought about how I would be looked at when I came into the rink the next day to teach 8-10 year olds how to play hockey, dealing with the rest of the staff, and word getting out to the parents. What if the director was scared to deal with parents that would not want their kids being coached by a "freak show?" Reality took over, and I chose to savor the positives of this magical night. I got close to campus and found an empty parking lot and changed my dress there while in the car, ever so reluctantly, and took my rice-filled nylons that made the perfect C-cup illusion of boobies out of my sweaty bra. Although my homemade art projects were very sweaty, a bit slimy and smelled of something that was sort of stale, I knew they were the most affirming item I had that night as I put them carefully onto the seat so they could dry out, figuring that no one would know what they were if they happened to look inside the car, and would never have any idea that those were the most valuable item that I could have had to pull my outfit together for the privilege of experiencing the most euphoric night of my life up to that point. The walk into the dorm and up the stairs was a mix of being more excited than I had ever been in my life, and being so pissed that I could not have this feeling of euphoria all the time. Something changed that night, and although I didn't see a path forward to make this feeling a reality, I also knew that something would absolutely have to change at some point, the part about feeling normal was impossible to ignore let alone pass up the chance. I simply could not go back to being the boring, introverted Clark Kent again. I had to find a way to become Lois.

Samantha felt the same way, and we went a couple of more times that summer, with the same treatment, feelings of euphoria, with an increasing acknowledgement that I had to look into making something happen. Thinking about Marian, Jade, and Alex, along with the visibility and machismo that surrounded me with my job and hockey background, I did not see a bridge from one to another.

The confusion got more complicated. Superballs that were bouncing against the concrete walls all over that vault appeared to be more like the larger and heavier lacrosse balls, with fairly loud music, loud metal music that I really cannot stand was blaring inside the vault. Besides that, it seemed I was inside the vault and was carrying its heaviness on my shoulders all at the same time. Jesus, I've got to get the hell out of here! And I freaking meant it.

17

SAFE SPACES: ESPIONAGE OR HIDING IN PLAIN SIGHT?

As the years went by, the vault kept getting more and more suffocating. I was getting a taste of what it was like to be myself while I was out of town, and it felt amazingly normal. But what about here? What about the place where I spend most of my time, you know, the other fifty weeks of the year. Although I have very little free time to myself, I needed the escape while I was in town. I would no longer wait a year until I would be out of town again to feel the euphoria that is 'being myself.' I needed much more of this.

Just how would I do this? I had a job which takes up a ton of time and I am on duty seven days a week, definitely more than a typical 40 hour work week with weekends off. I was at all of the Union College Varsity women's and men's hockey games, which do not occur during the work week but on weekends. That, and being at some of other sports on campus, along with the programs that I operate on behalf of the rink on Saturday mornings and Wednesday nights. There are others, like coaching the women's club hockey team on Thursday nights and random weekends, and the Mustangs, an adult women's recreational hockey team which started out as a rink program on Sunday nights, and a youth recreational program on Sunday afternoons. Oh yeah, I coached my daughter's youth hockey teams for eight years before she went to prep school, and once she went to Canterbury School in CT, we tried to make the two hour and fifteen minute drive as much as we could to see her play soccer, hockey, and lacrosse. Add officiating hockey games to this schedule, which either happen on Saturday afternoons of Sunday mornings, and Monday nights. Tuesday night was one night I was at home, which was the night we reserved for Marian and I to watch "This Is Us."

Random Person: "Are You freaking kidding me? How do you get yourself mixed up with so much? One night a week with your wife?"

Me: I know. Just writing all of this makes me sick and helps me to realize what I should have all along: that I cannot be everything to everyone. The rink programs were part of my job to bring in money for the department, and while some of the coaching through the years was on my own, I did it since there was some payment from the officiating and some from the coaching, and because I liked it, and because the people generally appreciated me. The officiating was for money, and I liked it enough to want to continue the side hustle year after year.

I was finding it difficult to find any type of sustained time for myself to explore and to be myself. And I literally didn't know how to do that, a circumstance made more complicated by not having a real end game. Marian's cancer diagnosis was a huge factor, and now that it has come back, care was beginning to increase.

Without realizing it, I took the blueprint I used for my time away and applied it to my places back home. Knowing it would be so much more difficult with the possibility of getting caught was exponentially higher, and the stakes were so much higher, both of getting caught, and of not taking the chances at all. I was getting to the point where I would be very unproductive in my real life living without the opportunities to be myself, even if for a small amount of time.

I began to search out places that appeared safe, and safe meant a lot of things. It had to have friendly, accepting people working with hopefully a very accepting manager, a friendly clientele, and somewhere no one would know who I was. I also needed someplace as inexpensive as I could find, as I could only use cash so Marian would not see a credit card bill with charges for women's clothes and shoes all over it.

It so happened that shopping in thrift stores, with an accepting staff, I could try on what I needed to, and even get advice on whether it looked good for me or not. It was also helpful that mostly women went clothes shopping, and especially where I was shopping, in the women's clothes stores and sections of stores, which was much less threatening than places where men usually hang out. I had checked out the Salvation Army and the Goodwill stores, and after a while I found a few second-hand and consignment stores. For the majority of time, I could find quality items for a fraction of the retail price, which enabled me to be able to pay cash since it required little. It also gave me a chance to try things out without the huge investment of clothes at retail stores.

I always had some type of backpack, sports bag, or satchel in which I would conceal some women's items: shoes, dresses or tops, skirts, some sort of make up and maybe a pair of clip on earrings, just in case I was able to find a place where I could go do some of my best undercover work. It was just a bit depressing that my undercover work was actually taking a short opportunity to be myself.

I was fortunate enough to find a few places where I met some incredibly nice and friendly people working that were not only accepting but also very helpful and empathetic to my situation. So much so that I was able to make friends with several of the people, and they went out of their way to make sure I was able to be as safe and happy as possible.

In Albany, I became a frequent visitor at the Plato's Closet and Clothes Mentor, stores that buy used clothes from customers and sell them, which shared management and were located two doors away from each other. My first time going to Plato's, I stopped in on the way to the gay bars in downtown Albany and I asked a young high school worker where I could find some sort of cardigan or cover up for a tank top that I was afraid to wear at the time, around 2016. She sent me to the back corner where they would be located. I am not sure if she sensed I was nervous, or just not used to doing this, but I was a clear cis dude looking at how to be inconspicuous while wearing a women's tank top. She came back to help me out, and asked me where I was going and why I needed what I needed. I told her, and she took the time to look around a couple of areas to find me one that not only fit but also was exactly the combination colors matching the rest of my outfit while being androgynous with a flair of femininity. Having never really dissected it prior to this point, I explained that I wanted the people who were queer to recognize that I was queer, and the straight cis people to think that I was a cis, straight person who just dressed a little edgy. This description became the look I was striving for until I eventually came out.

I became a regular at this store based on the selection and prices. The Clothes Mentor store operated with the same business plan where people sell their used clothes to them at a low price and the store sells it at a slightly higher price, but lower than retail. Plato's is definitely a store for younger people, the high school and college age/young adult crowd, where the Clothes Mentor was more for mature women. Both had items I was interested in, and the workers worked at both places, and they were easy to get to know and be friendly with. It was more than a safe place, but a place I really felt at home at, so much so that the manager, knowing my predicament of gathering too many clothes to hide in my limited hiding spaces, allowed me to bring a bin into the store and store my clothes in the back room that I would not be wearing in their off-season. I had no problem trying on clothes in either of these stores, and also felt comfortable asking the staff about looks and/or fit. They were honest, and cared about my dignity enough to not sell me something that would make me look awkward.

At this point in this journey I never thought I would ever be able to go stealth, or to be able to go through life free of being discovered while I am dressed, either pre or post transformation. I felt that I had too many identifying male features, but I felt I could somehow live as myself. Getting to know Genn, the owner of Fifi's consignment store in the Albany area, really gave me the feeling that I could be closer to passing than I ever thought I could. Her store carried high end clothing and accessories, and she and her assistant managers were more than helpful. After a while, they knew what I was looking for, and knew right where to send me in the store if there was a particular piece of clothing that would work for me. Again, they were very concerned for my safety, which was highlighted at a time when an intoxicated man came into the store while I was in the dressing room area. I heard some commotion in the front, and the girls at the desk were telling him he could not stay if he wasn't shopping. The Assistant Manager came back to the dressing room area and mentioned that I should stay back in this area, since the man up front was drunk and seemed danger-ous, as they did not know how he would react to me trying on women's clothing. I felt it was the sweetest thing that someone has done for me, but at that time I was actually ready to get dressed and go out there to help them out.

Genn had to close the store during the pandemic, but much later after I came out she opened another business, which was a passion of hers: being a make-up artist. She is very talented with makeup and hair, and I followed her over to her new place for a makeup tutorial. She was looking for one of us to 'model' for her to show the group how to apply certain products. Of course, I was all over it and it was another life changer for a lot of reasons. One, even though there were no requirements or tryouts, I had never been a model for anything before and thoroughly enjoyed the experience of an expert make-up artist showing everyone how to make someone beautiful. I just needed to be willing, and before my transition I would not have been willing to put myself out there for anything, and was happy that I was able to expose myself for others to look at, even though Genn was the attraction. I also learned how to do certain things with my own makeup, was able to be assessed for the proper makeup shades and colors for my skin tones, and was able to order some things for myself. The most immediate takeaway was that I looked amazing. It was my first professional makeover.

Just like in the bars, any store or coffee shops I went into I looked around the parking lot for cars, looked at the people going in and out of the stores for someone I know, or someone who would not like my type and may be dangerous. When I got into the store, I did the same thing. I felt like a Secret Agent looking at the venue before the most important person themselves came in: Me. I eyeballed every person I saw to see if they looked familiar. I had a couple of close calls, and one of them happened in Style Encore, a place just like Clothes Mentor for mature women. I would go there, and again made friends by talking to the workers. I would go there often, especially once I got to know some of the staff. They seemed to enjoy seeing someone like myself so enthusiastic about getting the proper piece, and made a fuss about my ability to put certain pieces together, either with what I walked in wearing or what I would try on. I felt at home here, and got to know many of the workers, some are still there for the last several years.

The frustrating thing would be driving twenty minutes and taking the time and effort to clear my schedule or to have the time to break away from my schedule, only to find someone I know at the store. This happened on two occasions, one at Fifi's and the other at Style. Me being caught at a women's clothes store would require a quick and believable story, one of which I did not have.

That was another frustrating aspect of my life, since I didn't have a lot of chances for this, and was just another reminder that anyone from the outside of the vault would never be allowed to know anything about the inside of it, and vice versa. The word that came to the front of my mind for the entire length of the drive back each time it happened as I drove home was "FUCK!"

The same situation applied to coffee shops, which were usually safe spaces, as well. I started at Starbucks in Albany before Marian's original cancer diagnosis, near the largest mall in the area, and near University at Albany, the largest college in the area. This place had two different entrances, so I could go there and sit near one of the exits, and get my drink and sit and get some work done. This place also had some queer kids working there, particularly a college-aged trans girl. She was considerably younger than I was, but she was much further ahead in her process. We often spoke about our situations and our plans, and she was a great kid. This was comforting, and everyone that worked there was incredibly welcoming and comforting to her and to me. I would check out every single person that walked into the place, ready for my escape if anyone I know happened to walk in. With all of these espionage tactics racing around my head, I am not sure I was able to get that much work done, but somehow I did, and convinced myself that this risk was worth it. In the final analysis, it was worth all of the stress, time, and risk to go into this establishment to be myself in a pair of heels, or a wig, or some makeup on, or clip on earrings, or anything that I could not wear in my mainstream life, and be by myself, and be able to get work done. These opportunities were few and far between, and if I had the chance, even for 45 minutes to an hour and a half, I would take that chance and appreciate it.

I began to check out Uncommon Grounds, a bagel and coffee shop near the University of Albany with a great chill vibe usually filled with college students. The staff often had lots of tattoos and piercings and dressed very edgy, and gave off the vibe that this is the place I could really feel comfortable. The staff would sometimes comment on whatever it was I was wearing, while most of the college students didn't make a big deal out of me. They treated me with the vibe that I was just one of them and I was just another customer. I felt incredibly comfortable. The bagel sandwiches are awesome, as are their soups and coffee drinks. I could not get enough of this place. I did have to walk out of there once when I spied one of the adult hockey players that I coach on Wednesday nights.

The Oh bar on Lark St, Albany is a small little neighborhood gay bar on a very artsy street. It was comfortable and affordable, even for me to go into dressed in any type of feminine clothes. I always felt safe and usually could find someone to talk to. I have met a few people there, and have stayed in touch with a couple of them. But most of all, it is a place where we can sit and talk and interact without having to scream at a person that is right next to you or a crowd so dense you cannot even move. I have learned a lot about myself and the LGBTQ community there. Further, I was treated well by the staff.

I would go to the other two gay bars, larger dance clubs, but by the time I was there, it was often populated by people half my age. Those two bars are across the street from one another and were easy to go to, but I could not go there regularly, and had a hard time talking to people there. I feel I grew out of it in a way, that the atmosphere being too young and charged up, possible drug scene, and periodic reckless behavior from many of the patrons.

One incident temporarily derailed my confidence for this. I walked into Rocks NightClub one night, where they were having their weekly drag show. Within the drag show that night was a beginner contest. The performer I was talking to encouraged me to get involved. Although I had never before wanted to perform, I felt like this was an opportunity to have someone else who knows makeup to help me with this. I did it, and the competition was one other guy, who was pressured into it by his several female friends.

He came on stage and stood there, not even lip syncing, with hairy legs and a scruffy start to a beard.

I went out and tried to lip sync to the song 'When Will I Be Loved?' by Linda Ronstadt. At this point, I had not really plugged into the music choices, and was so nervous that I wanted to do this to a song that I knew the words to, and one I knew was short so I could get done with this as quickly as possible.

Well, you can guess the winner of a drag contest between someone who entered the building with a black and white striped dress and 4 inch heels against a dude with hair all over him who did nothing to perform. You guess right: him. Kicked my ass, I did not stand a chance. I knew no one in this place and had hardly any applause for me, while he had tons of energy on his side with his friends. It was a tough loss, and not very encouraging for someone who hoped to live as a woman someday, with a dream of modeling somewhere down the line. That was humiliating, but part of it was fun and very helpful for me to step out of my comfort zone and try to perform a bit. It also reinforced that I was not really excited about being a drag queen and performing, and I knew that was not my future.

18

SCARIEST MOMENT: UH OH!

In March, 2018, I officiated a hockey game in Bethlehem, NY that ended around 10:00 pm on a Friday night. Following the game, my referee partner and I took turns using the shower, and I of course got dressed as my normal, ordinary boring self. Once in the car and out of the parking lot, I began changing into a blouse and skirt while driving down Delaware Ave to the Oh bar. This change was happening WHILE I was driving, and I had heels on as well, although that was the last item put on.

I parked on the street where the bar is, went into the pizza shop two doors up on the corner to get two slices to bring to the Oh bar since they do not serve food. After eating the slices, consuming one beer, and talking to a few people totalling up to about 45 minutes, I began driving home by way of I-90 through the cross gates in Albany, where I-90 and I-87 intersect, and one of them is a toll highway. There was a large toll booth area where cars would have to stop to pay, or slow down if they have e-zpass and the lanes go from three lanes to roughly twelve lanes. Undressing and dressing back to my original clothes as usual while driving home, the same as I did on the way there, I was getting more and more frustrated having to change back into the cis-het male costume I was all too familiar with. I only took minimal items off, strictly because I wanted to keep them on as long as possible.

Random Person: Jesus Christ, Bri, what were you thinking? Changing in the car while driving? What would happen if you had an accident?

Me: I just told you what I was thinking and I honestly needed these 45 minutes or whatever time I could get to be comfortable, and had to change back so I would not be caught by my family. I mentioned I began to wait to change back because I wanted my time in as myself to last longer. I justified this decision as a safety concern, and staying in my dress was secondary. I realize now this was not true, and may not have been the best idea.

Random Person: What if you were stopped by police?

Me: I'll tell you exactly what happened when I got stopped by a cop.

The second I saw flashing lights I became NERVOUS AF! When I realized they were for me, I was extremely terrified. So many things were going through my head. This is not the way I wanted to come out, still wearing a blue skirt, blouse, and heels. I quickly removed my shoes in case I had to get out and do "the walk."

In total panic mode, but trying to convince myself not to panic and stay cool, so many thoughts come and go from my mind in five seconds: How do I tell Marian? What if I spent a night in jail & cannot coach Jade's team the next morning, how do I face the parents? How do I face the kids? I let them down. How do I tell Jim at work? I have to be at the rink around 8:30 am for a learn-to-skate class that I run. A state trooper stopped me, and I know several state troopers, do they post these arrests so all the troopers can see them? This is how they are going to find out? I can't afford this financially AND otherwise. But, a few deep breaths, and I realized I can do it, one beer will not make me drunk, besides I had two pizza slices. But, Jesus Fucking Christ, A DWI? I work in an athletic department! We tell the student-athletes all the time that you represent the college at all times, I'll lose my freaking job. It will be in the paper, and it will mention a 'man dressed like a woman' was arrested for DWI. It was freezing outside, I had a skirt on, and I had a small jacket on with a blouse. Never in my life was I ever that nervous that my legs were uncontrollably shaking with my knees banging against the steering wheel and each other. Perhaps the scariest, I could not figure out if he pulled over Clark, Superman, or Lois. I was wishing it was Jimmy Olson, the young copy boy in the Daily Planet's office.

He asked me if I knew why he pulled me over, to which I answered that I did not know, assuming it was because he thought I was swerving, because I knew I was not speeding. I may have been swerving a bit, I don't know, since I may have started to undress as I am driving, so by the time I get home, I am back to normal. As I always do, I start my way home as Supergirl, I pull into the driveway as Clark Kent.

"You changed lanes back there without signaling!" he said in a heavily breathed voice, as if I just committed a heinous crime. It's the crossgates toll plaza for Christ sake, everyone moves out of a lane and into another lane at that point. "I have to ask you to get out of the car please?"

I replied, "Can I ask why?" in the friendliest, most confident and sober voice I could come up with.

"Behavior like that suggests that you may have been drinking" he shot back a bit more sternly.

I told him exactly what I did, exactly what I ate and drank after the game, even the part where I change clothes on the way home so I don't get caught, and that I really cannot afford to be caught like this by my wife, or anyone I really know. I sometimes change on the way home, but I do not drink and am very careful when I do, and I could lose my job.

"You did not signal, I have to do this," he informed me. Which I knew was bullshit.

I did the walk, intentionally stopping myself from shaking with my hands from both nerves and from the cold temperature. This was late March, and freezing at that time of night. I remember it was below 32 degrees, but with a breeze to add to the nerves and discomfort, I was shaking more than I have ever shaken in my life. It seemed like it took ten minutes but I would doubt it took that long. I nailed all of the instructions, but those were ten difficult and terrifying minutes. I felt the mental toughness kick in, and remember what I was thinking–closing minutes in goal of a one-goal game, with the lead, I knew I needed to be ready for anything, as if my life depended on it. I also thought of all the soccer games as a kid, freezing in the late fall and early winter months trying to win a championship, just trying to stay tough enough to get through it. I needed every bit of mental toughness at this pivotal point in my life, as I also realized that I did not drink much and I ate, and can do these silly exercises, even though they are not natural movements. I knew what mental toughness was all about, and if athletics really gets you ready for the real world, this is where it had better freaking work!

After he allowed me back in the car, I was relieved, but still had to stick around. I was hoping the family was asleep, it was after midnight by this time after all, but the chemo made Marian's sleep schedule nocturnal at times. I know I did everything properly during his test, but it was not over until he said I can go. If he says he has to take me in, it is obviously not over.

The officer came back to my window, and this time said he needed a breathalyzer test. I hurriedly tried to remember if I should refuse, or if I needed to take it. Which one would benefit me more legally? I figured I had nothing to hide, and I took it. He then looked at it, and said, "You are perfect, no problem. Sit here and wait, you are going to get a ticket," and off he went back to his car.

Really? A ticket? Small price to pay for what could have been a DUI? I knew I did not deserve that. Being outed? HUGE Relief. Thank god. As I was driving home, I remember thinking that I needed to come up with a plan for this, and soon. I do not want to go over this again. I drove home TERRIFIED about what could have happened had I been outed. I also could not help thinking about what would happen if I DIDN'T come out. The fifteen minute drive home was very, very relieving and distressed at the same time.

Two other items from this experience: I went to contest the ticket and the Assistant DA gave me probation for three months. He was definitely fair, and he almost apologized for having to come in for failure to signal. It's pretty clear I received a ticket to justify the second officer's role in this nightmare. While pulled over, the officer who returned to issue the ticket wasn't the one who initially stopped me or conducted the tests; it was another who had arrived later and remained in his car throughout most of the ordeal. He was polite enough, but it was clear he'd come over more out of curiosity than duty, to get a closer look at the 'man in a skirt.'

But back to the being outed part? WOW! My life as I knew it would be over, although I was actually hoping for that. But this is not how I expected it to be over. How can I face Marian, who I love and have loved from the first time I saw her, when I walked past her and her friend, who I happened to know. Possibly she would stay with me, but this is not the way I wanted her to find out. The kids, oh my god, would hate me, and surely would be embarrassed to be around me; I would surely be out of their lives, which would be devastating. What would I say to the parents of all the kids that I have coached? And the kids? I would let them all down, so many of them looked up to me, and this would ruin all of that. That bothered me to no end, and I thought this way for quite some time afterwards.

I did not want to think about work–the campus and the athletic department--if I was forced out like this. In my head I saw each persons' face and how they would treat me, and had nightmares right then and there about how I would be ridiculed and disre-spected to my face on a regular basis. The student-athletes would have a field day on me, at least the male ones, and going to work would be a nightmare each day, like a kid getting bullied at school. I was one of them, a former college athlete, inducted into both my high school hockey team and my college halls of fame, a coach of kids and adults for most of my adult life, wearing a skirt? I had lived my entire life in athletics and exhibited all of the toxic masculinity that a dude should, and I love athletics. How can I possibly ever live like this and also meet the needs of the other person occupying my brain and my body?

I had to do something, and needed to take the next step. But what is that? I did not know exactly what this was going on inside me for all my life, and thus did not have a clear end game. No clue, but I had better do something...but what? So it was status quo. I exhaled, was actually proud that I handled this well, from the outside anyway, even though inside I was a mess. I moved on, but with increased concern that my day of reckoning was coming, and I was not close to being ready for it. I also did not change clothes in the car while driving; this was the end of that stupidity. That was the longest twenty minute car ride home that night.

19

HERE WE GO AGAIN - GOTTA GET GOING

Boston-Logan Airport, after spending the day meeting with a doctor at Dana-Farber, a leading cancer research hospital. I was waiting to fly back to Ohio, where I happened to be working a hockey camp at Kent. A couple of months earlier, we had noticed a lump on the side of Marian's neck, which the local doctors diagnosed the enlarged lymph node as Stage IV colon cancer in the lymphatic system. She drove out to Boston with her brother, and I met them at the airport to get a ride to get a second opinion from Dana-Farber.

We were hoping for some sort of good news, anything other than the same terminal cancer diagnosis. Friends, her siblings, and her father were telling us that there may be so many clinical studies out there that she could try and be cured. We were hoping the same thing, and that it would play out just like we had hoped.

Here at this hospital, some of the most brilliant minds in the world would study the disease and figure out ways to beat it, and we were told that the people from back home were correct--that the enlarged lymph node was, indeed, cancerous, advanced, and there was no known cure. They also agreed that the treatment, which was chemo, minus one of the most aggressive medicines that was in her previous cocktail, was the most effective for her condition to keep the disease at bay for as long as possible in hopes some other cure can be found. Not having this particular medication mixed in would make her treatments less painful and debilitating, which we savored as the most positive of the news we had heard. We both acknowledged that we knew what was coming, but I kept it together and did my best to attend to her emotions at the time, which at that point were neutral at best. I just wanted to be there for her, that is all I could do. I felt like I could at least make her feel loved and comfortable, and make sure she knew I would be there for whatever she needed for as long as she needed.

Back to Logan Airport. Waiting for my flight I was by myself, along with thousands of travelers, and began to ball my eyes out thinking about what we had just heard. This was it, the beginning of the end. I did my best to comfort her, but I could not imagine what she was feeling while digesting that finalizing news. I realized I was a mess, just a complete mess, no longer able to process what we had just heard and what was going to sooner or later happen. During the first round of treatments, I was determined that I would be there for her, physically and emotionally, and get her through that ordeal, cured and ready for her next phase of life. Roughly nine months earlier, she survived that round and could experience the euphoria that comes with the opportunity to ring the bell at the New York Oncology Hematology when she was declared cancer-free.

This experience was drastically different. There would be no ringing the bell, no excitement to accompany a happy ending. We needed a plan, and whatever plan I came to realize had to include addressing the need for help with my mental health. I needed to get my head straightened out, whatever that meant, so I could be present for Marian during what was going to happen with her for however long that would be, hopefully, a long, long time. At the same time I needed to balance my work duties to be able to provide for the family while I was keeping her comfortable and as healthy as possible both physically and emotionally.

The longer I waited for my flight, the more empty and distraught I felt, and the more on the verge of tears I was. With my best friend and my support system being the one I need to support, I called my next closest option, my mom. I told her of the diagnosis and let her know I was not feeling right, and have not for a while. I was always under the impression that depression and anxiety ran in her side of the family, and that has to be somewhat what I had been feeling.

Coincidentally, I had been thinking about this lately, with the mental health awareness program that our Women's hockey team supports with a theme game each year. Year after year the Union Women's Hockey team has a theme game called the "Do it for Darin" game, named after a youth hockey player and former teammate of one of the Union women's players, who died by suicide as a teenager. Each year, I helped out a bit with the setup of the event, donated to the cause, and after that it basically came and went like any other game. Yet that made me think much harder about the intended awareness. A month following that game, while watching a hockey game on Canadian TV, I listened to a game analyst on the game, a former NHL goalie. He was back to work on the broadcast after a long hiatus. He was discussing, in detail, about how he took the time off of his broadcasting duties on a major Canadian TV network to take care of his mental health issues, and that it saved his life. He was putting himself out there, on national TV, and felt great about it, not ashamed of it. At this point in time, I was beginning to think that mental health therapy was only for the people that need it, as I once thought that other people need mental health therapy, not me. I was now realizing that I was one of the people that needed it. If this former professional player could do it with his multi-national TV platform and his notoriety, I can do it with the extremely little bit of notoriety that I have on my scale.

My mom told me that, yes, she has been dealing with a couple of mental health issues for her adult life and is on meds for it. I did not know how to even start this process; I was totally lost. She advised me to start with my primary care physician and ask them to come up with a diagnosis, maybe some sort of a treatment plan, or refer me to someone more qualified. I made an appointment as soon as I could, which was the very next day from hockey camp in Kent, Ohio.

I visited Dr. M, and let her know that I was having issues with my mental health. After filling her in on Marian's diagnosis and my difficulty dealing with it, and answering a long list of her questions, she determined that I have ADHD, and likely anxiety. She told me she would treat me for both situations.

I had been comfortable with her up to that point and was immediately comfortable with her, and was more than comfortable to say to her, "There is something else going on here. I am having confusion with my gender. I think I am trans. I am trans. I think I am trans. I feel like a woman, I felt like this for a long time, and I cannot handle it anymore."

"Oh ok, that is great. Do you have a name that you would like to be called?" she said in the most conversational tone of voice, as if this did not shock her. It startled the hell out of me that I could even say it in a setting where I was in my everyday life.

"Brianne. B-R-I-A-N-N-E." I said, spelling it out in the most confident tone of voice I have ever spoken in. I realized before the conversation was over that this was the first person who knew both of my names. She handed me a referral for a social worker so I could have access to counseling, and it led to the best and most well known trans-competent counseling center in the area. On the next visit, Dr. M had all of my records in my file changed to name me Brianne. With my name not yet legally changed, they could not go all the way with it, stopping short with billing and anything financial. The staff all refer to me as Brianne, and I had never felt so comfortable anywhere in my regular life to that point. A slight cool breeze began to mix with the stuffy air inside the vault, making it more comfortable to breathe, more so than I could ever remember in the last fifty or so years. And like that, I remember thinking how relaxed I was and that I am on my way out. Knowing there was an incredible amount of work to do, I was on the way into a place I never thought I could go.

20

TO BUST OUT OF THIS VAULT, I NEED AN ACCOMPLICE

THE SOCIAL WORKER PROMPTLY REFERRED ME TO Choices Counseling and Consultation in Albany, NY. During the initial intake consultation over the phone, the therapist explained that she would call me Brianne, and asked how to pronounce it. She also explained that she would have to refer to me as my dead-name when it came time for billing, since my name was not legally changed, among a lot of other questions for clerical purposes. After the phone call for the intake, I could not wait to go to my first session in person and thought every day about what this therapist would say. I had never been so excited for a meeting in my life. I was nervous, realizing that my last two attempts at therapy were a total bust around a decade earlier. Back then I was checking into my situation to try to figure something out by any way other than therapy, but in those days, just like in the stores and gay bars, I had to pay cash for therapy. Even though I had insurance, I did not want to take the chance that Marian would find out that I had a therapist and have proof with the insurance documentation. I found the cheapest people I could find since I had to pay cash.

Luckily, one of those two ineffective therapists worked at the same place as I was going this time around, which happened to have a very long waiting list. Since I was a previous client, I was able to get in right away rather than languish on a waiting list for god knows how long. The previous therapy, while not being valuable for what it was, opened the door for me to get in this time right away. Everything sounded great so far and this therapist sounded very friendly over the phone; I just could not wait to start.

I dressed up for this first appointment in the usual way-by changing my outfit as I was driving the twenty minute drive to Albany, and the anticipation was really killing me. I had a dress, heels, and a purse, clip-on earrings, and a light jacket. I was so excited, I couldn't wait to tell her my story, and even if I got cold feet and could not tell the story, she could see my story by the way I was dressed. I had no idea what would happen; would she tell me I was out of my mind and that my symptoms are not like trans girls? Would she tell me what I should do, just like the other weaker therapists had done when they thought they knew what I should do and told me to go out and just do it or not do it? Would she tell me I am worthy and the most well-situated trans woman candidate? Would she tell me I had better quit trying to dress up in public during the day because I look ridiculous or might get caught, in an accident, or both? I had no idea, all I knew is that I was going for it. All in. No more slumping away from this opportunity like I did at the Laverne Cox event. I would not deny myself the chance to escape this vault by not telling my secrets, my story about who I was. I realized what this day meant, and I knew it would somehow change everything, in some direction. Which direction, I did not know, but I had the feeling it was going to trend toward the positive.

Sitting in the waiting room for around seven long minutes, out walks the person who would turn out to be the most positive person I had ever met, as well as the most important person in my life. who came from around the corner and said, "Hi, are you Brianne? I'm Carolynn."

From the very first few minutes, I somehow felt like I could trust Carolynn to tell her anything, although some things were still difficult to say out loud. She spoke to me as if I was normal, and as soon as she explained that I didn't have the language to understand what I was feeling while I was a kid, or even as a young adult, it became obvious to me what I was doing there, and I felt more and more comfortable as the session went on. She sat there comfortably on a large chair, sometimes sitting on her leg that was underneath her, as if we were just two girls in a dorm room chatting away about everything. The things I would tell her, which seemed so difficult to verbalize, such as I would change clothes on my way to a bar, and change back while driving back home, that I was hiding a lot of clothes from my wife who I loved since the day we met, or that I would underdress-wearing women's clothes under my own clothing, got easier and easier to say the more I continued to talk. By the time it was over, I was so relieved, and also disappointed that I had so much more to tell, and I could have sat there and talked all day. But that is not how it works. We were allotted an hour and I floated out of that office, and although I had to change clothes again on the way back home I felt a lot more like a normal person.

I was realizing as time went along that at no time did I feel judged by Carolynn, ever. I looked forward to meeting with her every week, and each time I felt more and more special, like I mattered, that what I was doing was not just some strange fantasy or some phase I was going through, like that was typically reported and echoed in my male world. This was critical since I had told her more and more each time, getting more and more vulnerable, yet simultaneously confident. I had a feeling that she really believed in me. The first thing that comes to my mind, among so many highlights, is the session three months in when I walked back to the room after going out to fill my water bottle and saw a young, maybe twelve year old kid in the lobby, looking a bit confused and nervous, with the appearance that they were used to being in this place. I made a comment to Carolynn regarding this kid along the lines that I wished I had this opportunity to be in this place as a kid their age. Carolynn quickly followed that by explaining that with my high profile and visible position on campus, my leadership positions from being a supervisor and mainly a coach, that I would be a great role model to others that are trying to figure themselves out and can significantly impact others that see me, greatly helping people like the kid out in the lobby and the college kids waiting for a chance to come out to be themselves. I have remembered that message and it comes to my mind often, very often. I will never forget it. It keeps me going with my personal mission to help all of the "next people" that need a role model–someone that can exhibit joy and happiness unintentionally and unconditionally.

Carolynn is the most positive person I have ever met, and I was totally comfortable to spill out anything I was thinking, including the aspects I was not proud of. She was the second person in the world that knew both of my names, and the first person to know so many intricate details about both of my worlds. She was the first person, including even best friends, family, or anybody, that I was able to let out my true and complete vulnerability, and she was/is the perfect person for this. That in and of itself has made my transition so easy and made me feel so comfortable, free and happy. Through the process, I often would thank her for making me what I am. She then explained that it was me, that I was the one who did the work and figured out who I was and how to get it done. I could not, however, have done any of it without the perfect person who understood me and my place within the times and my places I was in previously, and that person understanding the culture of the time periods that she was not even alive for. Previous counselors never seemed to be able to resist throwing some judgment in there, which stalled things to a halt and essentially aborted the entire relationship. This does not mean she was afraid to step in and tell me what I needed to hear, which was sometimes difficult, and would challenge me to think and plan what would happen. Those instances were perfectly timed. I could not have gotten through that difficulty without her positivity, trust and belief in me that instilled the confidence that I could be my best self. She says it was me who discovered all of this about myself, but she will never talk me out of the importance of this confidence that she instilled in me as a person. I realized that I could and should be an open book, telling everything about my story, and was able to be that with her, and later, with the world. I am and will be forever grateful.

I went into the first meeting with Carolynn trying to figure out how to manage both of my "selves." Before long, she helped me figure out that I could not do that and that I had to come out. I felt like I could talk to her like I would talk to a friend. I walked out of each meeting not only knowing that I had learned lessons that I needed to learn, along with gaining the confidence that I could be who I know I am by her words and her sincerity. We also shared the belief that I could legitimately touch others and make a difference.

I looked forward to meeting with Carolynn each time the same way I did when I looked forward to every youth hockey game or college game I played, which was with great enthusiasm and confidence, and that it was the most important thing to happen to me not only for that entire week, but the most important thing to happen to me up to that point in my life. She also told me that it was me that figured it out on my own, that she simply gave me ideas to figure out my course of action. I know she was the catalyst of it all, and set it all to motion. (We actually argue this point each time it comes up-and I KNOW I am correct on this point) Among my favorite people on earth, and has such a gift at being her and doing what she does. Having Carolynn in my life was very much like having been granted visiting rights in the vault, where I could only be with one person for an hour per week, so I had to find the most perfect person I could possibly dream of for this critical work. There is no doubt whatsoever that I found that perfect person with the knowledge, skills, and empathy that provided the perfect chemistry to work flawlessly with. She was perfect, and I knew I would be not just ok but that I could handle anything life throws at me.

21

LOOK OUT, I'M COMING

COMING OUT. COMING OUT? HOLY SMOKES, NOW I really have to do this coming out business, which would be a considerable amount of work if it was to work out in the most positive way. Luckily for me, Carolynn is in the business of helping people strategize their process of coming out. I was looking forward to it and visualizing it for quite a while now. At the same time, the actual act of coming out was new to me, and was not as easy as just saying I am trans and moving on. I KNEW there would be some difficult conversations, and I felt as prepared as I was ever going to be. This is the most terrifying experience that will ever happen since absolutely everyone who I have ever known, met, or who has ever seen me will know about this change, and I would be judged in one way or another by all of those people, along with everyone I come into contact with. I realized I was not at the same stature as Caitlin Jenner who was known around the world for winning the Olympic Decathlon gold medal at the 1972 Olympics, and was famous for being a reality TV star on one of the most popular shows on television. However, when I started to think about everyone who would find out, would be everyone I had ever gone to school with, played on a sports team with, extended family members, anyone in the hockey communities at the various places that I lived, anyone I had coached, both adult and youth, the people I worked with, and the number of people is staggering.

Just about everyone that I spoke with has similar aspects of their coming out stories. Three themes came from these conversations and I knew I was prepared to tackle them. The themes are as follows:

1) **Controlling my message.** It was my story to tell, and I knew the message needed to be rolled out incrementally. My message needed to be something that was truly authentic to me and allowed me to set the stage and maintain my boundaries. To me, the more support I had, the better. I did not want the people I loved, trusted, and were closest to me to find this out through the grapevine. I wanted for those people to hear it directly from me.

2) **Identifying my support system.** Marian needed to be the first to know, and I intended to spend as much time as needed with her and the kids to help them to understand this situation. My support system is my immediate family. We were already supporting Marian through cancer treatment, and I had a hunch, at least hoping that Marian and the kids could be there for me. I need to be there for her and the kids at this time and in the future. My kids, followed by my parents, my closest friends and the people I worked with needed to be next in that order.

3) **Determining my strategy with my extended support system.** Here comes another difficult part. The people outside my immediate support system need a bit of a different approach. This is a first impression I would only get to do this once. I need to organize and deliver the message efficiently, effectively, and with supreme confidence. I could not waiver in this, I needed 100% conviction on this to each person I spoke with since any type of apprehension would make them question if I am for real and I was not just doing this for attention, or experimenting, or any of the reasons those who do not approve of this concept would suspect. I

needed a consistent message since this would soon be out on the rumor mill with messages being changed and judgments accompanying every single time the story was shared by anyone. I would not be able to control it once it got past the first few important ones that I could trust to keep a secret, so I had to do this with absolute certainty.

My approach focused on getting those superior to me at work on board. Support needs to come from the top down. Those ranking higher than me at work need to know exactly what is going on. It was critical to have their "blessing," and their support, so I can have the backing, and the "credibility" to come out to all others, including the people that work for me. I needed to consider how I would approach our coaching staff in our department, some of whom are in the LGBTQ community but others were known for their noticeable hegemonic masculinity. In addition to coaches, I work with folks in other campus departments, including blue-collar employees who help maintain our facilities where the default is to engage in toxic masculinity.

Marian was the first person to know and it was Sunday, March 31, 2019, the morning after watching the movie Bohemian Rhapsody, the story of the band Queen and their lead singer Freddie Mercury's life and his struggles dealing with love and his sexuality. We were up on Sunday morning, talking about the movie we both enjoyed. "It's crazy that unisex clothes were all the rage in the 70s, and believe me, I saw a lot on my brother!" my wife pointed out in a non-judgmental way.

She admired Mercury's life partner for accepting Freddie as he was. Yet, we talked about how Freddie was to blame for ruining his relationship, and at the same time he struggled so much with his secret. Marian mentioned her brother, who had identified as gay all of his life, and how the family had all kinds of problems trying to keep his sexuality a secret from others on the Air Force base that they were stationed at in West Germany in the late 70s and early '80s. Mercury was a pioneer in that he had no problem telling the world, yet her brother was pressured to hide his secret for fear that it would ruin his father's career in the Air Force.

I blurted out, "I am feeling the exact same way. I am trans, I have to do it, I am transitioning. I can't take it anymore."

After a couple seconds of silence, I followed up with "I've been getting counseling, I have finally decided that this is what I have to do."

A few more seconds of silence. I added, "I need to be more present for you and a better friend and partner than I have been the last several years, or decades, really. I love you. I still love you, and this is the only way I can get my head together to be able to be there for you."

After a few more seconds of silence, I continued with, "My name I chose is Brianne, B-R-I-A-N-N-E."

Her reaction suggested that it was not a complete surprise. Marian must have noticed my clothing choices seriously changed, and that my hair was getting a bit longer up top while still shaving the sides, giving me a more androgynous look. The conversation took over two hours in the kitchen, and at the end of the discussion, the takeaway was that I needed to do it at that particular time to be more present for her during her fight with cancer, and to be a better partner, parent, and just a better person. Marian deserved more. With things spinning inside my head like they were, I felt myself becoming gradually distant, and I couldn't accept that. We had also not been sexually active for several years; and often didn't sleep in the same bed for the last few years, due to a lot of factors. These factors include my line of work and officiating schedule typically involved late night hours, and I often need the TV to help me get to sleep. Like her mother, she experienced early menopause, which likely contributed to the vanishing of sex and likely the separate sleeping quarters. Her chemo treatments put an end to any type of sexual activity.

She understood what I was saying and was initially agreeable, although she was not thrilled at not having her husband by her side as we got older, but at least we would be together as partners. It was a surprisingly easy conversation to have, with the transition into the conversation writing itself (pun not intended).

She was immediately heavily involved with the strategies of coming out to the kids. She even started to pick a name out, one that started with the letter A, since that was the first initial of my deadname and she liked the initials AB. She came up with a bunch of possibilities, Amanda, Amelia, Ali, Allison."

In my first difficult part of a conversation, I stopped her and told her that I had picked out my name, and that I have settled on that one. I told her that I had always liked the name Brianna, a lot, but I dismissed it since I coached a player with that name. I did not want to make it look like I was naming myself after a youth player I coached for fear that the parents would think it may mean more than just my new name, that there was a more intentional reason. All kinds of these thoughts came to my mind about these situations. I continued to tell her that I was at Starbucks a few months ago to get a decaf mocha, and they needed a name to write on the cup. I blurted out the name Brianne. This was literally the first time I thought of this name, but in the moment, I figured it could be a french name, and if a hater or someone or anyone I knew came in, I would be covered. But, I realized the part about someone I knew, well, then I would have to come up with something else, like I was getting this for a friend named Brianne. I realize I did not think that one through at that split second, but I did find a name that I felt was made for me.

It was as if the vault I was carrying on the top of my neck all these years was dropped, and I felt like I was breathing the outside air, the air outside of the vault. And for the first time, I vacated the tight confines of the vault. I was not only in fresh air, but I finally got to stretch out my legs. I got to step out and walk around for a few minutes. I knew I had to step back in the vault, but this time, I knew the combination for it, and it was available as soon as I was ready to use it for good. It was among the best days of my life, and I have been grateful for her understanding reaction ever since.

Later that afternoon, the transfeminine support group I was in was having a hair and makeup tutorial hosted at the salon of the hairdresser of our group leader. I met Tom, the owner, who recently lost his wife, a trans woman named Gigi. Only four of us trans girls from the group showed up, and there was so much personal attention toward each of us. They gave me ideas of what could happen to my hair and some makeup tips, and I left with so much confidence and hope. It was amazing to know that there are professionals in the beauty and wellness world that care about us, that realize we need a little help since we did not get this through experience or through being taught by friends or family at a younger age. I have stayed in touch as my hair has grown long, had my hair colored and straightened more than once, and their advice has been invaluable.

Driving home that afternoon, I realized that my lives were beginning to merge. I felt my conversation with Marian, telling her my new name and my plans on the same day as I was learning how to take care of my new self was amazing. I was no longer hiding from the most important person in my world. That day was the start of both of my worlds coming together. This experience at the salon following coming out to Marian made this by far the most invigorating day of my life up to that point.

I called my friend Samantha from Akron to let her in on my elation and euphoria. She was so happy, I felt as though I was being hugged over the phone. She knew how amazing I felt to get the heavy burden off of my chest. She then said, "It is fitting that you came out to her today and that all of this happened on Trans Day of Visibility!"

"What is that?" I asked.

"Yep, today is Trans Day of Visibility, March 31."

"Wow, that is so ironic." I was on such a high at that point, and

I did not want the night to end. What an amazing feeling, one I am not sure I could ever forget.

At that point, Marian was willing to assist me in telling the kids, and we started with Jade, our sixteen year old daughter. She was away at boarding school at the time, and we waited roughly five weeks to get around to telling her. On a Saturday in early May, Marian and I took what appeared to be a random day trip to see Jade, take her to dinner, and hope to find a time to interject the news into the conversation. This appeared rather easy to bring up, as if she knew what was going on. She was teasing me about my distressed jeans, and my top with a wide scoop neck. She actually brought that up as soon as she saw me, but I was not ready to dive into a life-changing conversation as soon as we arrived. However, I did not have an avenue to bring it up during dinner without an abrupt change of tone.

After dinner, when we were bringing her back to her dorm, she went on teasing me again about my look, saying that hopefully no one sees me in this get-up.

I asked, "What would they say?"

She stuttered a bit, trying to come up with something to say, then replied, "Probably that you look like a girl."

I replied quickly "Jade, What if that is true?"

Crickets from the back seat. For more than a few seconds, there were no words from any of us to break the ever-emerging uncomfortable silence.

"What do you mean?" she finally replied.

I started with, "I love you more than anyone in the world, and you are the most important person to me in the world, and have been since we picked you up as a baby."

I knew I needed to continue right now or I would lose my nerve, so I continued, "I need to transition; it is something that I have been going through my entire life, wrestling with for a long time. With everything going on with your mother's health, I feel I need to do this now to be there for the family, and be a better person, more productive at work, and a better parent to you kids, and a better partner to your mother. I need to be there for her and this is the only way I could. I realize this is a lot for you, I just can't go on with this bottled up inside me anymore, and I need to be there for your mother, and for you kids."

She was silently crying, trying to suppress her feelings.

Marian noticed and mentioned, "Jade, it is ok to be sad, and mad and emotional. It is ok to have questions."

After a brief pause, she added, "I do not quite like it myself and wish it would not happen, but I understand that something needed to be done, that your father has to do this to be well."

After sitting a while longer, roughly five minutes, Jade muttered, "Can I come back home with you tonight?"

Marian got out of the car and into the back seat, where she said, "Yes, we can take you, but you have to come back tomorrow, and your father will have to drive you since I could not handle the drive two days in a row."

We drove home with Marian in the back seat, cuddling with Jade the entire way back. Jade was devastated. It was the single worst day of my life, and there is no close second. I have never forgotten the day we went to New York City to pick up the beautiful little child that we adopted and developed a bond with over the last sixteen years, which changed my life for the better. I was completely devastated knowing I had just shattered one of the people I care most about in the world, and I knew I needed to help fix this.

Jade did not talk to me until the car ride the next day, until she stammered, "Your outfit is cute."

I was wearing a pair of tight sweat pants with a tight t-shirt and a lightweight hoodie over it. I felt the warmest feeling at that moment, I didn't really expect it.

She asked, "Are you going to do anything with your voice?"

I immediately said, "Yes, yes I plan to yes." Even though I did not know exactly what as of that moment, other than that I have been cruising YouTube for ideas. I kind of thought she would be ok with it after adjusting to it, but it was not for her. It was relatively quiet the rest of the two and a half hour drive down there, and while I felt good about the conversation and then compliment, I felt really uneasy about her acceptance going forward. Would I spend the rest of my life wondering if she truly accepts me for who I am or would this be a point of conflict? It remains the worst part about the entire journey.

22

BRANCHING OUT

I THOUGHT THE NEXT PERSON THAT NEEDED TO KNOW was my mother, but following Carolynn's suggestion, I decided to call my brothers so they could be allies and possibly be there when I called my mom. Both of my brothers live within twenty minutes from my parents' house where we grew up. I called Darren first. He and I had always been close, and we have very similar interests, and felt I could talk to him about pretty much anything. Well, we will find out about that. I felt like these conversations may be easier the more of them I do, but that is before I start, and each one I realize they have absolutely no idea what is going on.

After a few days of thinking about it, and coming up with an excuse after excuse each night of why I could not call him, I made my mind up after six days of waiting around. That one night, when no one was at the rink, I called. The ice was not in, and with no one around, I brought Baron, my highly active German Shepherd, to throw tennis balls for him on the concrete floor and get him some exercise since the ice was not in. I would throw the ball down the rink, and he would run and retrieve it, then jog back to me so I could throw it again inside this quiet yet echo-filled building, the dry air making me thirsty. Throw after throw I tried to come out to Darren. After what seemed like an eternity of small talk I finally blurted out, "Hey, I actually have something to tell you. I have been struggling a lot with my gender, actually, all through my life. I have been in therapy, and I figured it out, and I am transitioning into a woman. This is something I have been working on for a long time. I am telling you this, among the first to know, and hope I can get your support."

After a bit of silence, he said, "Wow, well, I don't know what to say, but I will support you, although I don't understand it all that much. But this will not go over well with mom!"

I quickly replied, "I realize that, although I believe I can talk her down. I think I can anyway, and I am going to tell her that I always thought I wanted to grow up to be like her, and I have struggled with this all my life. I knew I could never admit it out loud, not in our family or in our world."

It was a long discussion. I told him I could not keep it in anymore, and I need to finally, after all this time, be myself. Mainly that I seemed to be more partial to emulating my mom rather than my dad, and although I took his persona as my own, I felt like I thought much more like my mother. I made Darren swear to secrecy, and told him if he needed to talk to please call me back, not to tell anyone else. I wanted to be the one to tell everyone else and did not want them to find out any other way. After a half hour of discussing this, he said, "I'll support you no matter what, but, I don't know, I believe if a person was born a man, then you are a man no matter what."

Feeling extremely exasperated after being slightly relieved, I simply answered, "You would not think that if you were in my body, in my head, especially if I did not know if I was a man or a woman, and I am asking that you trust what I am saying."

After a couple of other questions, he said, "This will not go over well with mom."

I came back and very confidently and optimistically said, "I realize that, but I will do my best to talk to her about this. I think it will go over better than we think."

I actually believed it.

He then brought up an interesting note, "You know, during our childhood, we, our family, did not say the words 'I love you' a lot or have any deep talks as a family."

I thought about it for several moments before I replied, "You are right, I know I didn't, but I don't know why. It was not that I did not love my family, but we just didn't say mushy things. But I love you, and I appreciate any support you can give."

It felt great to say that, as I did not even begin to say "I love you" to my dad until recently. I made up my mind right then and there to change that, that it's ok to say mushy stuff. I didn't even say that type of thing all the time to Marian, and I regret that.

Darren reciprocated, "I love you, and I will be there when you call mom. I would call Grant pretty soon if I were you, so we can both be there." I did not bring up being at the house when I called her, it was thankfully his idea.

Grant was next. This call was easier, as I was not as close to Grant as I was to Darren, if only because Grant and I did not share a lot of common interests and hobbies to talk about. I gave the same opening script as I did Darren, and he just took it in and said, "Ok, that's ok. I'll support you." He then added, "Mom will be pissed, and yeah, she will be pissed."

I replied with, "I spoke with Darren and he said he would go to mom and dad's when I call them; would you be willing to do that with him? The solidarity would help."

I felt that was good, it was a much shorter discussion, and basically no questions that I can remember him asking. I asked him, "Please keep this quiet, do not tell anyone, I do not want the word to get to them before I tell them. They should not hear this through the grapevine."

"No problem." He replied. The next morning I received the

nicest text from his daughter, my niece, who was a freshman in college at the time.

The text read,

Hi! This is Morgan by the way, in case you do not have my number. My dad told us about your news yesterday and I just wanted to say how happy I am for you that you are taking this step towards living the life you want to. I hope this transition goes as smoothly as possible for you! I can't begin to imagine how difficult this situation must be and I don't expect you to talk about it especially with your niece but I just wanted to let you know that I support your decision and if there's ever anything I can do to help you and the family let me know (I'm only a broke college kid but if there's something I can do I'd be happy to do it.)

I also wanted to ask how you'll be spelling your name?

Anyway, love all you guys and hope to see you guys this Christmas! 🤍

Wow, this is just what I needed. Morgan has always been a sweetheart, and to have someone so directly having my back in the family was the best feeling at that particular time. It took me a bit to realize that I had asked her father not to tell anyone, and he wasted no time telling his family. I knew I had to get busy and tell my mother, but I know no one really wanted to be the one to do that.

It took me a week after giving the news to my brothers to have the nerve to talk to my mother. I was really relieved that they decided to be at the house when I called, not only for the support that they can give me by telling them they are on board with this, but most of all so that held me accountable to not drag out this process. It took a few days as it was for me to get around to setting up the call, and I had to arrange for both of them to be there, it had to fit within their schedules. I knew once it was in motion, I had to go through with it. This was going to be THE most difficult phone call I have ever made, and I could not delay it anymore, and waste my brothers' time.

I was nervous AF. I dreaded this one for three days, as soon as I had it scheduled. This could either go really well, and she will be touched that her little boy needs her now more than ever, or, she could absolutely hate it and think I need mental health checked right away.

I knew this one would take a while. I knew we could only do a bit of small talk since my brothers were going to be there, so I jumped right to it, as confidently as I could, "I need to tell you something, something serious. You know I have been taking care of my mental health since we spoke about it, and I have figured out what I need to do. I have the anxiety and depression piece taken care of, and there was also a piece I did not tell you about, and it is my gender. I have found out that I have to transition into a woman."

Pause.

"Huuhhh?" from the other end.

"Yes, I realize now that I have to do this, that my mental health has been affected by this for the longest time, ever since I could remember actually, since I was a little kid. And all through my life."

In a stern voice, she said, "You are my boy, you were born my little boy, you are not a …woman!"

"I realize this is difficult. The truth is, I did not know what it was, and did a lot to explore this, and finally figured it out. The truth is, I actually thought as a kid I wanted to grow up like you, but I also wanted to play hockey in college. I wanted that more than anything, but I realized I actually want to be you. I feel you were the perfect mother, a great role model, and I wanted to be like you. I love you, and I want to be like you, and I hope you can support me ."

Silence.

She allowed me to talk and answer her questions, which I did not anticipate, I actually was ready for an explosion and a huge argument. After a couple of other questions, about how Marian and the kids took the news, she came up with, "How much of this is because of what happened with you and your hockey coach while you were in high school?"

"None of it. It has nothing to do with it at all. In fact, these types of thoughts started as soon as I could remember, about five years old," I replied, "In fact, nothing happened anyway. I know his reputation was bad and I knew his act, but I stayed clear of all of that."

Yes, I am still lying through my teeth about that experience, just as I had done all through my life. But I did not lie a bit about that experience being a nonfactor in my transition. It did not in any way. Your biological sex has nothing to do with your sexual orientation, or who you want to sleep with. People that are gender nonconforming can be attracted to anyone or everyone, the same as cis people can.

"Besides, this happened way before any of that, I was wearing your shoes and your old dresses when I was the only one home, and that was way before I knew him."

"Reeaallly? I never knew that"

"I can't believe you did not know, actually, I was actually afraid I would damage one of your pairs of heels, black strappy pair," I replied in a casual, conversational, matter of fact tone of voice as if we were just two girls reminiscing.

"I had no idea," she replied in a surprised tone of voice.

"Bras sometimes, nylons sometimes," I continued

"Wow, I had no idea."

"Honestly, I thought you may have, mothers always seem to know everything."

The actual call, which was over two hours, was exhausting, and emotional, as I told her all the same messages that I told Jade, Marian, and my brothers, and told her a lot of what I had to hide all my life. Topics that kept coming up were the interactions with my coach, in which I never did clarify that there was inappropriate activity actually happening, but made it clear that me transitioning had nothing to do with any of that. As a mother, she was on to that, which did not surprise me a bit. I knew it had nothing to do with the conversation at hand. I just did not want to muddy up the waters. The one here she did not know I used to wear her clothes, well, that one surprised me, not only the thought that mothers know everything, but there were times I just got everything put back where they belonged as my brothers were coming up the steps, already inside the house. I must have done a good job, which surprises me that I can put everything that I had on my body back where they all belonged, which were in three different rooms in the house in under a minute, yet I did not properly straighten my own room when I stored my own clothes. She just could not come to terms with the difference between gender and sex. She actually listened to what I was saying and did not really argue all that much. I could tell that she did not agree with it, but I thought it just may work.

It was a relatively civil call. By the time it was over, I was emotionally drained and had no more energy remaining to talk to my dad, but my brothers were filling him in while I was on the phone with my mom. Darren told me they stayed a long while after it to talk about it after she got off of the phone. While I was a bit relieved that it did not come to yelling or disowning me, his prediction came to fruition as it turned out, she did not take it very well at all. About a week later, Marian sent out a bunch of pictures to the family via text, as a way to keep them informed of what is going on with us, with us not living nearby like my brothers and their families do. I received a voicemail from my dad, saying in a stern tone, "Do not send any pictures of you to us. You look horrible! Not everyone is on board, like you say they are, no one here likes it!"

Long Silence. Click.

Well, that one was admittedly tough to take, a bit devastating actually. During the time between the conversation with my mom and my dad's voicemail, I had heard from both of my sister-in-laws, my brother's wives, to tell me they are proud of me and support me. I realize it would take my parents some time to process. It would be a long time until I would speak to them by phone again. This was May, and the next time was Christmas, which is a long time.

Alex would take a while to tell. He still had a month or so of school remaining, and we were waiting to tell him until his school year was over to avoid a huge distraction at the end of the school year. This meant I had to wait until the Union College term was over to come out on campus, since I did not want Alex to find out from the grapevine either. When it was time to tell him, it was not the perseverance of the concept that we predicted. Well, it was, but in a positive direction. He was eager to hear more, and I suggested that he could come with me to see Carolynn, and she could help explain things to him.

Alex came with me to my appointment the next day, and Carolynn could not have been nicer to him, and he to her. He mentioned a couple of times that he doesn't know anything about this, and is worried about my "transgender appearance." He said he would support me and help others understand my situation.

Jade and Alex tried to make things work, and Alex really tried hard. He had just been reconnecting to his old friends that lived across the street and a couple of houses down. The family has always been very religious, and were with the very conservative Ukrainian Catholic Church, where Alex had been joining them for Sunday masses. The parents would only refer to me by my dead-name when I would call them, something I would not allow. I called one time to ask where Alex was, and the mother answered the phone, "Ah Hello?"

"Hi Trish (not her real name), this is Brianne, I need to speak with Alex, it's really important."

She came back with "Oh Hi [DEADNAME], yeah he is over here"

"It's Brianne, you know what my name is, I even said it! You are just being a bigot about this, and I need to speak to Al right now, it is important, it is about his mother."

"I'll get him," she muttered nervously.

When Alex answered the phone, I said, "Al, is she right there? She is an absolute bigot, and I need you to come home right now. Your mother needs you."

Alex, sensing how upset I was, said, "Dad, please don't say those words around me, she may be able to hear."

"I hope she freaking hears it! I do not care. Trish is a bigot, and so is Paul (not his real name), he is more so. Your mother needs you to get home now!"

After a couple of back and forths about why he should come home, I was more livid by the minute thinking about how they just blatantly avoid calling me by my name. Classic transphobic people who hide their hate behind their religion, and Paul is a deacon in his church, where he shielded himself from any blame for all of his hate.

I realize this puts a strain on Alex, as he tries to be friends with all of them. As an Autistic kid, he does not have many friends that are his peers and he is very friendly to his teachers and other adults. I have backed off, but not after him sharing his conversation with Paul about why he would not call me by my name. Alex had a talk with them about his wish for them to support me, and their response was something along the lines of "would you call a tulip a daisy?" in an attempt to make a ridiculous comparison. I have agreed to not interact with them, and he is still influenced by their bigotry in the disguise of their lord jesus christ, the guy they believed who welcomed everyone into his world, including all outcasts in society.

23
DEAR COLLEAGUES

THE NEXT PART OF THE PLAN WAS TO SIMULTANEOUSLY come out to my department, and other colleagues at the college. I knew I could not just show up in my favorite dress and say, 'Here I am, my Name is Brianne, Let's do this!' I knew there had to be an order to it; certain people had to know first, and I wanted to tell as many of the people that I was close to and that I worked the most with first so they would not hear it from the grapevine; however, I felt it was critical that I received support from my supervisors above all others. This way, when word starts to travel, I know that my bosses heard the news from me first, and they can make sure that any information that was needed to be shared would be done accurately and with respect and professionalism. Above all of that, I trusted them, which made this entire experience a very slight bit more comfortable in my mind.

When I say that the experience was slightly more comfortable, I mean slightly more comfortable than if a wild bear was thrown into my vault and the door locked behind it. I was terrified. I trusted them, however, and I was dying to get this out, but actually sitting down in front of someone that has power over me that I had never discussed the subject matter with previously was terrifying to say the least. Up to that point, I had told two people that I knew I could rely on, our Administrative Assistant, who was a recent Union graduate, and a sincere person. I needed someone to talk to about this, and I got the idea for the letter that I would eventually send would be written by me, but from her email, so it would be my letter and my words. I felt this to be a good course of action since she often sends department-wide emails. I also felt a bit awkward sending it from myself, thinking in my mind that it would look as if I had departmental backup if it came as a bit of a more official correspondence.

The other person who knew my secret was my good friend Kelli, who works in the office right next to me, and is by far the friendliest person I know. We sit and laugh all day long, and we talk about family happenings. She was such a sympathetic ear while going through Marian's entire cancer journey, and I knew I could trust her. The fact that she would be the first to see me every day and would comment on how much she liked a vest or shoes was uplifting and affirming, especially before saying anything. It was comforting to know that she had my back on this entire venture.

But it was time to get to work, so I could eventually be comfortably out at work. I first approached Joanne, our Senior Associate Athletic Director and someone that people can confide in in her office and asked if she had a few minutes to talk. She said "Sure, sit down, what's going on?"

"I wanted to tell you first. I know I can trust you. You probably can sense this, but I am having issues with my gender."

I then thought quickly in my head that I got this and I am going to just rip the band aid right off and spill it.

"I am transitioning into a woman. It has been going on for a while, but I am getting ready. I figured you would understand, and I knew you should be the first to know."

Joanne smiled "I knew something was up, with the way you

had been dressing, but I did not want to bring it up to you. I wanted to wait until you were ready to disclose."

I immediately felt like a couple of the dials on the front of the vault were turned, and my shoulders felt free. I am not sure what I said at that point, but I told her I felt so much better and appreciated the chance to talk about it.

She then said, "Can I give you a hug? This is great, I am proud of you!"

I melted at that very point. Jo is someone whose opinion I had always valued as long as I was at Union, and I learned so much from her and felt indebted to her at that moment.

We spoke for another 45 minutes or so, and I felt amazing, very much at ease, wishing I could just go out there right now and be me. Then she said, "So when are you going to tell Jim?"

"Do I have to? Couldn't you do that for me?" I joked. I then continued, "I intend to when I can pin him down for a while, I have a feeling it may be a longer meeting and I know he is busy at this time of year."

Well, half joked. I knew I needed to talk to Jim about this, but boy, wouldn't be nice if she could do that for me? But I knew the news absolutely needed to come from me, and despite how much I dreaded this interaction, I was actually looking forward to it, at least getting it out to him and getting past this. Jim is a terrific Athletic Director, and a great leader. I have learned a great deal from him and it has always been clear that he cared about all of the members of our department, from coaches to administrators to support staff, and most definitely, the student-athletes. He had never done anything or had said anything that would make me think that he would not support anyone in my situation. However, my situation had me locked up in a vault with a lot of messages generated inside my brain going back and forth, and a conflicting message from what I just mentioned is that he was a football player, a fraternity brother, and most basic of all, a dude. I kept going back and forth with these possible outcomes, from the point of view that he was the consummate professional to the point of view that considers his past as a part of a culture of the toxic masculinity cesspool. I was literally up all night before I was to speak with him in his office, I mean not a minute of sleep.

Despite me being nervous AF, I went in feeling surprisingly confident. I pulled the band aid right off, saying "I am sure you are wondering about my changes lately, and I want to tell you that it is that I have been figuring out my gender and I am transitioning to a woman. This has been going on for such a long time, practically all of my life, and I needed to do something so I can be a better partner and caregiver to my wife, a better person and be better around here."

"My name is Brianne. I would appreciate your support on this."

"Wow, that is great. I did not see this coming," he said, seemingly searching for something to say, as if he had never been in this situation before. Then, as he always seems to do, came up with the proper question, "What can I do to support you?"

This time, it was my turn to not know what to say. I did not have a great answer for this. I had only thought about how I would come out, and what I would say to everyone I would discuss with, how I would write my email to the public, and to whom I would include. But what could he do to support me? The best I could come up with was, "Just please use my name, and treat me like you always would."

"The way I see it, I see it as, everything being normal, like nothing will change"

"Business as usual" I attempted to clarify.

"Yes, business as usual," he agreed.

The chat could not have gone better, and I felt more and more confident early in the meeting and as I filled him in on who knew and who else I would tell and when I would tell them, I felt the load on my shoulders even lighter.

"I realize I may look rather weird or awkward, and you may get questions about me. I really appreciate your support, thanks so much!" I said as I floated out of the office, smiling at our Administrative Assistant mouthing the words "it went great." Her gigantic grin said it all as I continued out to the office and into the next parts of the process. I had a comforting feeling that things would work out on campus, still with a ton of work and more discomfort, but I had the people that I felt believed in me and my story, and believed in me as a person and a professional.

As the time went along, there were now four people who knew, along with Beth, who learned from Jim and Jo, and I was thankful for that. Beth is such a great person, and I never had the guts to let her know that I see her as brilliant at what she does, and how much I look up to her as a colleague, an administrator, and a woman. I did not realize it before, but I began to recognize that she has been a role model for me this entire time.

There were others in our department subsequent to this point in time, through early June 2019. Cheryl is our long-time Head Athletic Trainer, and someone that I talk with from time to time, usually with her stopping up to my office to chat about what is coming up, and discuss ways to handle issues that happen to come up. One day, she stopped up in the outer office where Kelli works, and checked her mailbox located right outside my door. She came into my office and sat down in my arena chair from the now defunct St. Louis Arena that is in my office for visitors. She made some small talk and asked a question that I would be pretty sure she either knew the answer to or did not really care to know, and after I answered it, she leaned toward me and said in a hushed tone, "I don't know what you are going through and you don't have to tell me but I am with you 100%." She slapped my knee and got up and walked out of the room and downstairs to her office inside the athletic training room.

This came a bit out of the blue, although it was not a surprise, since Cheryl has a huge heart and loves to help people. Throughout her thirty plus years at Union as the Head Athletic Trainer, and among the first female head athletic trainers in college athletics, she is respected and revered by all of the athletes and staff alike. Although I was stunned a bit, a feeling of warmth came over me when I instantly realized someone saw I was awkward and something serious or special (or both) was going on and cared enough to reach out and offer support without knowing the exact scoop for rumor mill fodder.

I was hoping she would have stayed there so I could tell her, but I finished up whatever it was I was doing, then called her and asked her if she wanted to come up so I could fill her in. I appreciated that she was able to come up right away, and I told her everything. I swore her to secrecy until I was able to let Alex know; we were keeping the news from him for about another month and a half until school was over out of fear that he would focus and dwell on this to the point that he would be completely disengaged from his regular life. It was great to talk about it and tell my story one more time, as it was getting easier and easier to talk about the more I spoke about it. It also felt good to help someone connect the dots regarding my approach, look, and style of dress. It felt great to add another person to that list of allies and supporters.

Kelly, our field hockey coach and another kind soul throughout her nine years at Union, approached me at my office one late afternoon as she was going downstairs to train some of our athletic teams in the weight room. She popped in and just said, "Hey there, I have been noticing that you seem to be going through something, and just wanted to let you know that I am a good listener, and if you ever wanted to talk about it, I am here."

This melted my heart. I was not sure if they were really coming up on their own, or was the story getting out, but I saw her a day or two later, and asked her to come in and I would fill her in. We talked about a lot of things, and to tell her my story, to someone who cared, and to tell the story one more time again made it easier to imagine me being able to tell people en masse, and to be able to tell other people in my own words, my own message being transmitted on my terms in my words about my feelings.

I was also thrilled to now have many people who knew and supported me, and with each new person that knew in the department, the better I felt that the majority would be supportive. I knew there were more difficult ones to tell coming up, along with the athletes, especially the male athletes, but for now I was happy that all was going according to plan.

24

ON THE TOP OF THE WORLD-
REBIRTH APRIL 30, 2019

ONE OF THE MOST ANTICIPATED AND BEST DAYS OF MY life was my 3:00 pm appointment with the endocrinologist. I swear I woke up each and every day in the month of April, which began the day after my euphoric day telling Marian the other part of my life's story. I dreamed about what it would feel like to have hormones running through my body. How different would I feel? How soon will my boobs grow? Would my genitals shrink? Once I had a breath of air outside of the vault, I could not think of anything else in anticipation of April 30, 2019. I didn't need a calendar pinned to my wall or a reminder on my phone, the date was etched in my memory. That date, time, and place was on the top of my brain the entire month.

I knew about the doctor's reputation for not having the best bedside manner, but everyone put up with it since he was the only endocrinologist in the area that treats transgender patients. I could not wait to get to the appointment at 3:00pm. After all of the work with Carolynn, the weekly therapy sessions, the heart-wrenching talks with my family, various co-workers and friends, putting together the plan, along with a timeline of when so many of the events would happen, this was it, THE day! I walked into the endocrinologist's office in my favorite teal, pink, and burgundy flowered dress, heels, and a smile on my face you could not wipe off of with a dirty rag. I felt new, reborn, and that was just walking into the building. No one would stop me now. I am all in. The excitement I exuded was tampered only by the slight worry about if for some reason, this would not be possible. I knew this day was different, and would change my life like no other day could.

I walked in as if I had been a woman my entire life, and I am not sure I had ever felt the type of confident feeling I had that day. I was weighed, and I told the nurse this was the most exciting day of my life. She smiled and said something about being glad that I am experiencing it, but I was too excited to really listen closely. She actually could have told me if I took the hormones that I was asking for that I would have a week to live and I honestly would not have known. Honestly, I am not sure I would have cared.

In the exam room by myself, I was told to change into a gown, which I could not wait to do. I took a selfie, because I wanted to mark this day. I did my best to keep my emotions in. The other options were Planned Parenthood who would treat trans people, and the Gender Wellness Center in Oneonta, NY, which has the reputation of one of the best transgender care facilities in the east, but was an hour away. I have the privilege of having insurance that covers transgender care, thanks to the work of Gretchel and our Human Resources department at Union. I was not the first employee to come out as trans, and I realize that the others prior to me had to fight for these considerations. I owe so much to Gretchel and to those who came out prior to me for all the work they did to pave the way for my smooth experience, all for the cost of a co-pay. Thinking about this and how lucky I was to be in this room, I had a lump in my throat and misting up of my eyes. I think of the people of the past and the present often with gratitude for so many of my experiences of my coming out journey.

The doctor finally came into the room, and he asked questions that had to do with therapy, and how long I had felt this way. He read the letter that Carolynn wrote recommending me for this treatment, which was required. He asked about my wife and family and how they accept my transition.

"Does it affect anything, what everyone else thinks? I am totally ready." I uttered as nicely as I could to the most important person in the future of my life, attempting to not upset him.

"No, not really, no." he replied "Just trying to get background."

After a couple of more questions, he asked to check my breasts, which he did. His next question made me the most nervous:

"What is your plan? Do you plan to have surgeries?"

Oh boy. I had heard so many different rumors, that they will not prescribe hormones without a firm commitment to have all of the gender affirming surgeries. I was nervous that if I did not answer in the affirmative that the deal would be off.

"Can you let me know a bit about the surgeries? I had heard a few things but I would like to hear from you how it all works."

This reply was to buy time just as much as it was to learn how the surgeries would actually go. He let me know that the top surgery was a bit risky but relatively easy compared to the bottom surgery.

In a tone of voice suggesting he has said this spiel every day of his professional life, "For bottom surgery, it is quite expensive, and the wait is around 18 months after you get the initial consult. You would need to go to Philadelphia, or maybe Montreal. It is very expensive. You would have to dilate daily, up to four times a day at first."

I replied, "I heard I would not be able to walk for a while and would have to dilate but did not know for how long."

"You would not be able to walk for about six weeks, and would have to dilate a lot at first, then taper it down. You would have to dilate for the rest of your life periodically."

My next question was on my mind this entire time. "Would I

need to commit to surgeries in order for you to prescribe hormones?"

"No."

"No? So I would not have to have any surgeries at all?"

He answered, "No, you don't have to do anything you don't want to do."

Every positive vibe came to the surface, and suddenly the vault was the most comfortable place I could ever be in, although I knew I was still in there. He then told me what I had been waiting to hear every single hour of every single day of the last thirty days.

"I am prescribing Estradiol, take one pill each day to start. 2 milligrams per day, which is one pill per day. They are little blue pills. I am also prescribing Spironolactone, which is a Testosterone blocker, you need to take two of these a day. You can take them both at one time, or one in the morning and one at night. Splitting them up may work better, but you can do either one, whichever is easier for you."

OMG! I was amazed, this was finally happening. I felt music envelop me, although I could not tell a particular song. I had never felt like this before.

"I will need to examine your genitals. Please slide your underwear down."

I was fine with this. He could do literally whatever he wanted with me at this point. I had no idea what was going on and it seemed reasonable to me. I got dressed, visualizing myself at CVS looking like the cutest little girl asking her mother for ice cream while asking for my new meds pharmacy counter. I left the office saying, "Thank you so much, I really appreciate this! This is such a game-changer!"

Game-changer? I really said that? Jesus, I could not come up with anything else? But that is what came up.

I was walking on air out of the office and could not wait to describe it to everyone. Walking out of the building, I was singing softly to myself the words to "On Top of the World," the Carpenters' version. At least the words I knew. I sang in my head, and to myself out loud, and could not get the song out of my head as I drove straight to the pharmacy to pick up the pills. The twenty-five minutes needed to get there seemed to stand still, it just didn't matter. I literally felt as though I floated into the store and straight into the line for the pharmacy counter. Just as I saw in my mind twenty-five minutes earlier, I was a cute, young little girl that could not wait for the best treat of my entire life.

Many of the pharmacists were used to me being there, and have seen my transformation as I was often there picking up scripts for myself and my family for the past fifteen years, and an increased amount in the previous two years since Marian had multiple scripts for all of her cancer treatments. The woman that showed me the meds leaned halfway over the counter and asked in a whisper, "Do you know what you are doing with these, do you know how to take them?"

I very quickly and proudly replied, "The doctor told me what to do, and I can't wait to start. It is also described here if I needed it, but seems pretty straightforward to me. Thanks so much."

"I am really happy for you, you will do just great!" she replied with a warm smile. I knew right then and there that she knew these directions were the easiest directions possible, and that I did not need her help. It was her way to tell me she was happy for me. Another small gesture contributing to the biggest day of my life.

I could not wait to go home and swallow these prized possessions that I have been craving for months. 5:35 pm. Somehow I felt like a real, live, legitimate woman at that moment. I knew I still had a lot to deal with the coming out process, but I felt normal. My insides felt normal. Between 3:00 pm and 5:35 pm, the direction of my life, and who I actually was, and who I would become, had changed for the best possible irreversible direction.

After living 'On top of the world' a couple of hours, it dawned on me that something was missing. I looked at my phone probably over fifty times looking for someone to call, or text, or somehow notify what had just happened. I could not share this extraordinary, life-changing experience with anyone. Marian knew it was happening, but with her sick with a life threatening, incurable disease, she would be excused if she was not quite as elated as I was. Carolynn was out with a family issue, and desperately wanting to tell the person most responsible for this success, I texted her anyway, knowing that no reply would come my way. I texted Samantha to let her know what had happened, and she replied with a heartfelt message. To make this process work out the best possible way, I had to stick to the plan and remain comfortable inside the vault for a couple of more months. I could now do it with a confident, new and exciting feeling.

One downside to this day actually presented itself four days later at a presentation by a trans expert representing our insurance company. During their talk, they told the nine of us attendees that if a doctor asks you to let him feel your genitals, tell him to "Go to hell, go "F" yourself! NO one needs to see your genitals, it is not part of the process, and he has no business with anything down there." His job is to provide hormonal care that could affect breast growth, and has nothing to do with genitals. Knowing this made me a bit sad that this doctor apparently took advantage of my naivety and my excitement for a little of his own pleasure. This bothered me for a long while, and after consulting with other trans women and experts on trans care, I heard different opinions on the caretaker's need to keep track of the genitals. I still feel uneasy about it, but not as upset as I was when I first heard this news. It was among the first incidents that a negative action by someone would taint an otherwise euphoric moment.

I had made up my mind that moving forward April 30, 2019, no one was going to knock me off of the 'top of the world.'

25

A MEMORIAL EXCHANGE

By Memorial Day, 2019, I had put in at least a year of work taking care of my mental health, spending time in therapy, and starting hormones. Having already been moving my wardrobe toward a more androgynous look throughout the year, I decided that I would take it to a bit of another level with my outfit, wearing a pair of royal blue skinny pants, a white tank top, and a light-weight long red blazer, with white canvas shoes. This look, for me, was stepping out, and I was wearing it to campus, as Memorial Day is a regular school day for our campus and I felt It was some-what safe to at least wear the colors of the good ole U.S. of A. But, we all know the real reason: an excuse to step out a bit and take a chance.

Around 8:50 am, I walked into the rink, and found myself about 25-30 feet behind four members of the women's hockey team. The team had been good to me, and several of the members had been very friendly, perhaps more friendly than they may have been over the years. Wearing this red, white, and blue outfit in the brightest shades possible, I would not blend in with the crowd wearing and I didn't really plan to. But I was not quite ready this early in the day, being only twenty seconds into the building, but with these women in the area I had to say to myself, "Well, here we go." I was hoping that they would keep walking. Instead, Cheyanne, among the most outgoing players, turned around and said, "Hey Brinker, I really love your outfit!"

WHAT! Jesus Christ, I swear I had no idea what to say. In my head in those two or three seconds, I wondered, did she really mean this? Was she teasing me? No, she would not do that, she is not the type that would embarrass the staff member who runs the rink that early in the morning. What the hell do I say now? I'd better think of something and say it now before it gets awkward and I embarrass myself. With those two to three seconds feeling like it was like fifteen to twenty years, I said, as confidently as I could, "Thanks, just getting into the holiday."

"Well I really like it, it looks great!" she came right back with, while the four of them were turning the corner on the way around the rink and into their locker room.

"Thanks so much, I appreciate it!" was my quick reply this time. At this point, my day was made, and I was literally floating around the rink on my way to my office. In my head, this exchange could have gone either way, but it could not have gone better. I had a couple of different places to go on campus that day, and I wanted to challenge myself. I figured that coming out day was coming up for me relatively soon, so I cannot get into too much trouble that I cannot get out of. I was amazed at how that made me feel; the rest of the day flew by, with my red, white and blue outfit all over campus. It was just a simple comment of her being nice, but I believe that they saw someone that was nervous AF, and had been going through something for the past few months. She made a comment in front of her friends to validate what I was doing, to make me feel comfortable with myself. Looking back it really was a mature thing to do, and I will always appreciate that twelve second exchange. That comment meant the world to me. It is amazing what a small gesture can do to lift a person up. Those twelve seconds came and went for Cheyanne and her teammates, but it significantly accelerated my coming out process and enhanced my comfort level on campus, giving me a feeling that I've got this. I can do this. The students are actually good with this. This moment, those few words, those brief seconds, essentially accelerated the process for the better.

Once I was out, the next time that the team or any students saw me was the following year, and to a player, they could not have been more nice and accepting. We spoke about clothes, boots, and things that girls talk with other girls about. I did not hesitate to ask any of them for advice for my outfit on certain days, particularly game days. Things like which pair of shoes should I wear with a certain outfit? (I often would bring more than one pair just in case) Should I go with the hat or not? Or should I tuck the top in or leave it out? They were very gracious and helpful, and even though I was still learning the finer points of fashion, I was confident enough to not be embarrassed to ask them. I was honored to drop the ceremonial first puck at their Do It For Daron game that year, the annual mental health awareness game. Led by the outstanding 2020 graduating class, the 2019-20 women's hockey team remains my single favorite Union College Athletics team I had dealt with in my eighteen years at Union, which says a lot since our Men's Hockey team won the 2014 NCAA Division I Hockey Championship, and one would think it would be almost impossible to top that. But they did.

26

SORRY I HAVE AVOIDED YOU

THE OFFICE OF INTERCULTURAL AFFAIRS (OIA) IS ONE aspect of the campus community that I could have never imagined myself interacting with, and I mean never. I had been doing my thing as an Assistant Athletic Director, watching over the varsity hockey games as the Event Administrator, scheduling all of the facilities, renting out our facilities to generate income and working with our teams and user groups. I was on the Safety team for the Environmental Health and Safety office, since I was in charge of upkeep of the facilities. I was also in the meetings of the Facilities Services Department, where I would act as a liaison to that department, exchanging information based on the needs of each department. Beyond that, I would handle requests of other departments when they needed to utilize our facilities for a campus program, and worked with them on their needs along with outside rental groups that used all of our facilities. My involvement with the rest of campus was rather limited prior to this, and I enjoyed interacting with other areas of campus. I feel I got along well with all of these people, who were great to work with.

Among other departments I did not interact a lot with prior to this, Residence Life, a lot of the academic areas, Admissions, Registrar, Bursar, and the Office of Intercultural Affairs. Really, what would a white, cis-presenting heterosexual male need to interact with the OIA, where in my own mind they dealt with students of color, foreign students, spiritual life and of course, the LGBTQ+ community. Gretchel, was the Dean of OIA at the time, and was someone I was in a couple of meetings with when our department was hiring a coach to confirm compliance with our interviewing process, but really never interacted with.

The meeting was relatively brief, yet informative. She was very welcoming, and after we went over things such as name changes and pronouns, she made sure I informed my supervisors, and Human Resources office about legal changes. My main reason for the meeting was to find out how to navigate the bathroom situation. Which bathrooms and locker room should I be in? Was there a campus policy? I shared, "I do not feel comfortable in the men's bathrooms anymore and I do not feel I belong in the women's bathrooms and locker rooms yet."

She comfortably told me, "You should continue to use the men's restrooms and once you are out publicly on campus, you can start to use the women's bathrooms."

I immediately thought I would belong here as a woman thanks to that brief exchange.

Fortunately for me, I had been able to use the officials locker room downstairs in the rink, which has a one-stall bathroom in it. This was perfect, a bathroom with privacy so I do not have to be seen in either of the others in that building. It also meant that I would like to use the single stall bathroom throughout campus if they are available. This was huge for someone in my position, and of others that essentially identify as neither of the two main genders. All I heard about was the "bathroom bills" that were being put forth in various states, such as North Carolina, making the bathroom situation more than a little bit uncomfortable. New York State had no such law, but while in my vault, I felt that the women would have a problem with me in the women's restroom on campus. It was not until I stepped out of the vault to ask this question was I comfortable with my timeline.

The refreshing part of this was the next part where she told me about the two people on campus who had transitioned previously and subsequently left the college. She had been there for those people and let me know that she had fought for transgender services to be covered by our employee insurance. She also informed me of the LGBTQ+ Affairs Committee on campus, which was made up of several unbelievably dedicated and brilliant people, and said she would recommend me to that group that I join. That suggestion jettisoned me to the very top of the confidence ladder. I was not sure why she would recommend me to this committee, which was full of faculty, staff, and students that have been working on enhancing LGBTQ+ issues for years. Amanda and Charles started this group around fifteen years prior, and I could not understand why they would want me on this committee, and actually felt funny attending my first meeting. I wondered what in the world I, a not even out yet trans woman with little to no experience of being out, can add to this group and the subject matter. I had so much to learn how to be out and how to navigate certain situations. But her mentioning that she would recommend me to the group made me feel incredible and legitimate, and for whatever the reason, I may possibly have some sort of avenue to enhance my visibility on campus and become the role model that Carolynn said I would be.

I was intimidated the first time I attended a meeting, and it happened to be the final LGBTQ Affairs committee meeting of the school year, feeling like such a non-expert among experts. These folks, the faculty and staff members and students alike, have been leaders in this community for several years, and have worked so hard to change the minds of administrations to enhance the experience of the LGBTQ+ community for year after year, and I showed up because I was invited by Gretchel, someone I had no real prior relationship with. The process that I navigated on campus was made significantly easier because of the work of these heroes, and what would I, nothing but the beneficiary of their efforts, be going to add to this group? I guess I did not feel as if I had earned my way in or had any credibility going into it.

Standing there as someone I was not, yet at the same time joining a group because of who I would become, was an uncomfortable situation to say the least, but very exciting. It was made much more comfortable once it started, seeing how the members of this group would interact and have fun with each other. These meetings were and continue to be the most enjoyable, relaxed, yet sensitive and informative meetings I attend. The first item we discussed was the Lavender ceremony, which is a ceremony for the self-identified LGBTQ+ students and allies on campus to be recognized, in a safe environment, with only the people they want to invite to be there. Parents who are accepting are invited, other parents who are not accepting would not know about it at all. It happens a couple of weeks or more prior to the campus commencement ceremony to avoid any unwanted exposure to parents and family. I listened and figured I had the details and was ready to attend this sensitive event.

I was still a bit unsure of where certain places were on campus, and very nervous the night I was to attend my first Lavender ceremony, featuring students who I really did not know. I thought I would try to make another step with myself after the Memorial Day outfit, and wear my androgynous outfit with heels to the Unity Lounge. I was a bit nervous, but ready and determined to show up. So I walked my way across campus with heels on, hoping I would not see anyone I knew until I reached my destination. On the other hand, I was somewhat ok since I was ready to come out soon and had been dressing more and more femme, and they will find out soon enough. The issue was: just where was my destination?

When I showed up at what I thought was the Unity Lounge in a house on campus, a room dedicated to the LGBTQ community where I once attended ally training, I saw no one there, except two guys who lived in that particular theme house. They said they did not see anyone there, and perhaps this was in the Unity Lounge on the third floor of the Campus Center, the very room I avoided for so long. I then walked back to the Campus Center, the epicenter of campus, where people go for a variety of reasons, feeling increasingly vulnerable each step closer to the building I took. I sheepishly entered the front door, and thankfully did not see a lot of people due to some of the offices being closed. Even though it was around dinner time and students could come in at any time, I very nervously climbed two flights of stairs to the third floor of the Campus Center as fast as I could in my heels, trying to not make noise while I was doing it. I arrived at the room, and again, no one was in that room. I was now really nervous. I walked back half relieved to not have to really expose myself, yet scared to expose myself to anyone else on my way back to my office where I could change clothes. I texted the Director of Multicultural Affairs, and he said the event was next week. EPIC FAIL! Not very good preparation. I put myself through this stress and anxiety for an event that was not happening until next week. I could not describe my emotions after this, but relief, frustration, and nervousness was definitely among them. At least if I got caught going to the actual event, I could possibly live with outing myself going to such an important event. Now, I would be outing myself as queer, stupid and unorganized at the same time, and precise organization was paramount to the success of this entire process.

Could I have written this stuff down? Or put it in my calendar on the phone? Or even look it up somewhere? Well, yes, I suppose I could do all of those things, but honestly, that is how much my head was spinning in this period of time with various emotions, such as suspense, excitement, anxiety, and exhilaration, among others. As much as I was in control of this process and executed the plan at each juncture, at times, especially these times before I officially came out on campus and still had one foot in the vault, and the other toe almost touching the floor outside it, I felt like such a complete hot mess.

The following week, I did it again, this time showing up to the correct room just in time to start, but no time to chat with anyone prior to starting. I was wearing the same outfit and took the same vulnerable path to the event, and walked in and found the spot tucked in the far back corner of the room, which required me to walk past the back half of the crowd of roughly 40 people. I did my usual room check of every person there and spotted a few people that I know. I was a bit worried at first, but once my heart began to slow down a bit, I was able to realize that these people are here either because they are queer, or because they were very much supportive of all of the queer people in the room, and since my style of dress had been visibly ever-changing the second half of the year, I really had nothing to worry about.

What I witnessed was validation, love, and joy unlike any I have seen before. I was blown away each time a student was called up to receive their cord for their cap and gown, and the moderators spoke a bit about the person. At that time, friends and allies that were present could speak to the individual in front of everyone in the room. The admiration was unbelievable. They would tell stories of how they have helped each other and inspired each other to be the person they have become.

Up to that point I had been in some vulnerable spaces with support groups, and inspirational spaces with another person or small group of people, but have not seen this in such a large space of about thirty people or so. I was profoundly inspired by this public validation, and was determined from that point on to take every opportunity to lift someone up, both personally and publicly when I had the chance. I took this courage from these students that have been through so much loss, self doubt, and trauma. Those young queer people were absolutely instrumental to my current ability to tell my story and lift anyone up. This is from a person who was uncomfortable saying the words "I love you" to anyone who was not my wife or my two children. I grew immeasurably that day, and I really do my best to find any and all students l that would like to be at the Lavender Ceremony each year, especially the athletes, who typically do not really participate with the queer community during their time at school so they would not miss out of this feeling of community and inclusion.

27

DEVELOPING THE COMING OUT LETTER, AND THE COURAGE TO USE IT

A CRITICAL PART OF CONTROLLING MY MESSAGE WAS THE letter, the coming out e-mail. I wrote it out, then revised it, then again, and again, and added things, probably twenty or thirty times between when I started to write it in mid-March and when I would send it in June. Since this needed to be perfect, I sent a copy to my friend Kelli, my friend and office neighbor in the rink with whom I talk and laugh with all day every day. I also approached our Administrative Assistant, who has a trans brother, and is also a sweetheart, a friend, and would be a good ally, and she has access to everyone's email addresses. I asked her to read it and let me know if there is anything I needed to change. After she said she loved it and found a typo, I had asked her if she would be ok to send this to the department, since I felt it may be less awkward than coming directly from me. To that point in mid-April, I had just told my wife on March 31, and told Joanne, Jim, Beth and a few others by mid-April, so I still had plenty of people to tell within the two-plus months until I actually sent the email out. I just wanted the letter to be ready to go, or as ready as I could make it at the time, since I knew the message I wanted to deliver but did not want to lose it from my brain. So I sat on that, knowing that I at least had that in the can that I could hit send, but I would likely make further adjustments as time moves along and I got smarter and had more of a handle on the gravity of what will happen on June 28, 2019.

Marian and I decided that Monday, June 24 will be when Alex's school year is over and we will tell him the news. We decided that we would tell him on a Monday, since school was over and we would be going to the Outer Banks on Friday with Marian's brother, and her divorced parents, who turned out to be transphobes. What could go wrong?

The last week in June, we spoke to Alex on a Monday, and although he had questions about my "transgender appearance," he agreed to go to my therapy session the next day to learn more so he could support me. The letter to the Athletic Staff and other Union College colleagues had been on my mind each day leading up to Friday. Should I do it today? I better look at it once more. I did that for Wednesday and Thursday. Friday came, and knowing I could not allow myself to carry this forward through the entire week-long vacation and the week at hockey camp that followed, I made a couple of last-minute changes and sent it over to her. I told her to wait until I got over there to read it and asked her to let me know if it is perfect.

Alex and I were set to drive to the Outer Banks that afternoon for our drive. I knew I wanted this taken care of by the time we departed. On my way over to the athletic office in the Alumni Gym, our Men's Lacrosse Coach for the last eleven years just recently retired. He was a man's man through and through, tough as they come and coached that way, but did he ever love his players. We've had some chats about Marian's cancer, and I knew he had a gigantic heart. But this was different. I had remembered a conversation we had about Caitlin Jenner around the time she was coming out and gaining a lot of publicity, and knowing what his thoughts were on that, which were questionable. I was wearing a pair of women's shorts that morning, with a tight little red t-shirt.

He was on his way to Boston for an alumni fundraising event, and he made a little joke about the shorts. I don't remember it exactly, but it was to say something like that they had a name for those back in the day, and I was too nervous to even listen. I giggled it off and went inside to worry about the email some more.

I had our Administrative Assistant read it one more time to see if it was perfect and she said it was. I was sure she was sick of the whole thing by this point. I felt incredibly nervous yet excited to get this done, and I waited a bit more, probably a half hour, then asked her to hit the send button. I waited in the office with my phone in hand, waiting to see if I got a reply from anyone. It was quiet, school was out and there was barely anyone there. In about ten minutes or less, Joanne came out of her office and let me know she received the email and said it sounded great, and she was happy. She asked me how I felt, and I did not know, other than as if I was 100 pounds lighter to have finally hit the send button, but also nervous for the first person to reply.

The letter that everyone read:

Athletic Department and Other Campus Colleagues,

You may have noticed some changes in my appearance within the last few months, if not over the last few years. I would like to address this in an effort to make everyone feel more comfortable with these changes.

Through a lifetime of questioning and exploration of my gender, along with serious medical considerations within my family, the importance of strong mental health became blatantly obvious and crucial for myself and my family. With this I was able to realize I could no longer hide who I am and live two different lives. Thus I have come to terms that I am transgender and have started Hormone Replacement Therapy (HRT) to transition into a woman.

I am absolutely excited about this and have never felt better in my life; I have realized that by simplifying my gender, my mind will be clearer and focused to become a better care-giver, spouse, parent, and representative of the department and Union College in general. I also realize that although I have done a lot of preparation for this, I have a lot of work to do and a lot to learn during the process. I have the support of my immediate and most of my extended family and ask for your support as well. For those who already know, and to those who have reached out, I cannot thank you enough for your unconditional support. This is something I never thought could ever happen, and you have made the process welcoming, comfortable, and easier than I could have ever imagined.

If you have any questions at all about this situation (or advice), I am happy to talk about this–I am 100% comfortable talking about it, and I am no longer embarrassed or scared–I am more uncomfortable hiding it. I know this will be an adjustment, but I hope that you will attempt to use my name, Brianne, (pronounced Bree-onne), and my pronouns (She, Her, Hers). For those who are already using or would be comfortable using AB, that is absolutely fine as well.

Other than that, it is business as usual. Thanks very much.

Brianne

The first reply over email would have to wait, because in the next two minutes the phone rang, and the name that popped up was, guess who? Our Men's Lacrosse coach, among the most old-school people in our department. I let it ring a few times before I slid the answer button over, and said in the most confident yet matter of fact voice I could come up with "Hello."

"AB-I just read your letter, this is so great. I am so happy for you. (I felt my stomach get 60 pounds lighter that very moment.) I am very proud of you, and I am behind you 100%. Here, talk to Stef (our ticket manager and his assistant coach), he is right here."

Stef was as friendly and classy as he always was, and gave the phone back to the coach. He said "Once again, I am so happy for you and I am proud of you. Good Man, See you later" I did not realize the good man part until later on in the day, when we were driving down to the Outer Banks, but I was convinced it was not intentional. I was just greatly relieved that it was a supportive call from someone that I thought would wait to even contact me, and was unsure how he would receive it. Looking back, it adds up to his character. I have seen him yell at a player as they were coming off of the field, then a minute later, he approached the same kid on the bench and hugged him and told him he believed in him. At any rate, subtract more tonnage off of my shoulders. The vault, which had been cracked open, is now wide open for me to dance right out of there. I was breathing differently, so much easier, as if I could actually inhale twice as much air in half of the effort of breathing as it took before. I was no longer breathing the difficult, stale air within the vault. I had fresh air. I was officially OUT! I let Alex drive from Albany all the way through Delaware, including the New York area, before I took over. I was not worried about anything. The next phase of my life was here, and I was here for it.

28

FIRST MEETING OUT

DURING THE NEXT FEW MONTHS AFTER MY VACATION, IN July, 2019, I was beyond ecstatic about my new name, my new identity on campus and the hockey world, and every single aspect of my life. I took advantage of my newly claimed identity and inserted myself throughout campus, getting to know more people, joining committees and interacting with different departments, most of those I had very little or no contact with prior to this metamorphosis. It was so euphoric looking at my new email address, and I happily got used to the new way I answered the office phone ("Athletics, this is Brianne"). It was such a treat to change my email signatures, zoom name, voicemail, and the like. I also had the opportunity to talk to many supporters, some being new acquaintances, while others being long-time colleagues to help them understand what I was going through, and to ease their worries and assure them that if they happen to make a mistake and call me by my former name or refer to me by my former pronouns I will not be insulted. I was feeling worthwhile every single day, and felt myself growing within myself and in the campus community at the same time.

For the past several years I have been attending a weekly meeting for a campus department which is heavily male dominated, with only two women in it. By July, 2019, there were now three women in it. Going to those meetings as someone not in the department is sometimes a bit stressful, especially when I need something. But this first one in July was different. I was nervous AF. It was my second day back on campus since coming out, but the first one was a Monday with minimal exposure to others. This one was the first day that I was out on campus in a meeting, particularly with this group, which is a mixture of blue collar and white collar employees. I was well aware from my recent observations that women were often dismissed a bit, despite their relatively high positions on the staffing chart. I needed to be myself, and by that, I could leave nothing to chance. I could not have anyone guessing who I was and what I was doing, they needed to KNOW who I was and what I was doing. I wore a dress, had some low heels, not much makeup (I was still learning makeup at this time, maybe a little eye shadow, mascara, and lipstick). I felt amazing and ready for this, and all of the possibilities that could possibly come up.

I walked in a bit late, and naturally, the only seat that was vacant was at the back of the room, forcing me to walk the entire length of the table and on display of the fourteen people in this meeting. I felt the white hot spotlight of many sets of eyes on me, and those that were not looking at me were purposely not looking to avoid staring. As I sat down, someone immediately slipped me a paper with the meeting agenda and said hi. The meeting went along like normal, but it was anything but normal inside my gray haired head. When it was my turn to talk about our departmental needs, I did so flawlessly, without any nervousness, and was in complete control. It felt great. While walking out of the room afterwards, a couple of people stopped me just to tell me that I looked nice, and that it was great to see me. All told I came in and kicked ass, and was bouncing out of there and into the day, thinking to myself, this may just be too easy. Until…

About three weeks later I was in a conversation with one of the other women in the room. She relayed that beforehand, when everyone was dragging in with their coffee and such someone began a conversation that took over along the lines of "What is he going to be wearing today?" or "What is RuPaul going to look like" and other types of ignorant put-downs. Hearing this immediately caused a huge lump someplace in my esophagus, and what seemed like a toilet flush down lower in my stomach. I was crushed.

She continued, saying she then loudly smacked her coffee mug down and said something along the lines of "We will not have this type of talk here. We will treat her professionally and with respect." At that point, the banter stopped in the room. Also, at that point of our conversation, a feeling of warmth came over the inside of me, knowing the scenario with all of the ignorant smearing by the men in the room, that someone had my back, stepped up and put an end to it. It apparently only took one person to shut it all down behind my back at least in a professional setting, and I have not heard one word of teasing to me personally. I am not naive enough to think that it still does not go on, but I have been treated as a professional ever since, actually able to get things with less haggling than what I had to go through before I came out. While some of the positive treatment I have experienced since coming out may have to do with my confidence, a lot of it likely had to do with that one gesture that someone saying that the behavior would not be tolerated. In a matter of moments, I went from being crushed to feeling elated that someone would defend me like that to a group of men, and my professional life was lifted to one of dignity.

29

OFFICIAL(S) WEDDING

I WAS INVITED TO MY FRIENDS JAMIE AND CAITLIN'S wedding in August, 2019. This would be the first time wearing a dress somewhere out socially, off campus, and in front of many people who I know that have not yet seen me, and I was beyond excited about it. Many of the attendees were fellow referees, who I have known for a long time, but none of whom had ever seen me in a bright turquoise and pink flowered print dress and four inch fuchsia pink stiletto pumps. Before I went, my friend Jen took me to her friend from the store she works at that morning and she did my make up, while teaching me how to do it myself. I had yet to be that dressed up with makeup, and had yet to feel as beautiful. I could not wait, I was looking forward to this opportunity for well over a week.

By the time I reached a parking lot, the only spots available were far across the lot, the furthest away from the door you could be. While the wedding party, all of which I knew, were outside taking pictures on the groom's side, I was by myself and felt the same way I felt when I used to drive to a store or a coffee shop dressed, and get scared I would know someone in there and be outed. I reminded myself that I was already out, and there was no going back now. How I handled myself in this walk across the lot, and how I handled myself inside with everyone else, would determine success or failure due to my level of confidence. At that point, Carolynn's words came back to me, when she once told me that I am ready, it is real and that I have my shit together better than anyone that comes into her room. That is all I needed. I was ready for that moment.

I made every effort to walk across the lot and into the building like I owned it, but was still terribly nervous inside my body. I walked just inside the Glen Sanders Mansion for the wedding and basically made my way to the rear of the seating area where I saw a bunch of people I know from hockey, many of which I coached in the adult hockey program. I said hi to them all, and to others walking to and fro. Each time I said hello to someone else was nerve racking, but after a couple of uncomfortable minutes, Anna-Maria came busting back from the front of the seating. She and her husband and I were friends for a long time, and he was a groomsman. I had not seen her in years, and I was at first very nervous and trying to figure out exactly who she was. She came back and hugged me, said her name and that it has been a while, and that I looked beautiful and loved my outfit. She was so excited that I was seated at her table, and said we would see each other later throughout the day. We hugged again, and that was all I needed to validate that Brianne was 'in the house.' That sixty seconds is all I needed to feel free. It was amazing, I will never forget her kindness, which was nothing but normal for AnnaMaria, and was an absolute game changer for that day, and for any and all situations moving forward.

Everything was comfortable from that point on. I saw enough people I knew and talked to them before the ceremony, afterwards at cocktail hour, during dinner and during the dancing social portion of the day. I had tons of compliments on my shoes and some on my dress. At the cocktail hour, I spoke with a friend, who we were family friends with. She is a lawyer with a queer daughter and we spoke about the new me, and how things were going for me. She then asked, "What are you going to do about your name change?"

Umm not sure. Change was on top of my brain, I did not really know how. She mentioned she knows someone who takes care of name changes for trans people, at times pro bono. I was intrigued, but I was still working on getting along in the world, mainly still coming out to scores of people I knew in situations exactly like I was in at that moment, seeing people for the first time, even though they actually know or have heard about what was going on with me.

"I know a lawyer friend that does this type of thing pro bono, if you qualify. I will send you his number and you can contact him."

Back to the shoes, which were awesome, the only item of women's clothing that I had spent more than $15.00 on ever to that point. Even the lady at the Aldo Outlet store said that she loved those shoes and that I owned them the second I tried them on. Those beauties stayed on that day from the minute I walked out of my house at 1pm to the minute I returned at 7pm. Because I could. I did not have to hide with heels and a dress on anymore, and I was going to savor every second of it, sore feet and all. Not only that, a couple of the older ladies actually thought I was cis. Those same people also thought I looked good for an older woman, but the part I took from that was that meant I looked like a cis woman, and they were shocked that I was once a guy. At that point, I'd take whatever wins I could get it. I was very happy for Jamie, a guy that I knew since he was a twelve year old kid that used to hang around the hockey games and later worked part time for us and also became an on-ice official in our league. I was very proud of him and his lovely wife Caitlin. It was a beautiful wedding and a very fun reception.

I will never forget this day for several reasons. One, the euphoria that I felt throughout that day and beyond, for being able to be myself, wearing a terrific outfit among many people that I had known for around fifteen years, and I was out of the vault-without being tethered to it in any way. The other reason is what the conversation with my lawyer friend did to lift me up both emotionally and personally. I subsequently did the paperwork for my legal name change, and when that paper with the order of the judge declaring my name Brianne Rose-Myers Brinker came in the mail, it was another special day, like no other, another rebirth. Now, I did not have anything to do with the vault anymore, not only did the three-foot door close and lock with me on the outside, but it also disappeared completely from anything I could ever think about anymore.

Going to the DMV with the paperwork saying my name is now Brianne Rose-Myers Brinker was a delight. I made sure my hair was done well and my make up was on point, since this picture is among the most important that I would take in my life to that point. When I was standing, waiting for the picture, I did not know if I could smile or not, as if I had forgotten all other trips to the DMV. As a new person, I asked the question since I was holding a huge smile inside of me. The lady taking the picture realized it was a name and gender change and knew this was special, said, "Go ahead, smile, this is your driver's license and your picture, go ahead, look happy!"

I did that for sure. I was amazed at how I felt when I saw this legal document with a picture of me with the largest smile possible. It was something I could not believe actually happened, yet finally, with this card as validation that I am actually who I need to be. Later when I received my updated social security card, an amazing feeling of warmth, satisfaction, and glory came over me. Even though I expected it, the social security number is what everyone reveres in this country, to be protected at all times, and needed for nearly everything legal. Now mine is here in print on that little blue card. I made it, and I will never give it back for any reason.

30
WHO AM I?

W HAT HAPPENED NEXT WITH THE OFFICE OF Intercultural Affairs was every bit as significant as my first interaction. Our Director of Multicultural Affairs was leaving the college for another opportunity, and Gretchel began a search for a replacement. As a member of the LGBTQ+ Affairs Committee I was able to be involved with the candidates' interviews along with other stakeholders of this position, such as spiritual life and others involved with student affairs on campus. Not only did I have the opportunity to meet all of the spiritual life directors on campus, which I had never had the chance to do, I was able to have very little interaction other than to hear from the candidates themselves in a panel interview. A very unique, professional, prepared, and impressive candidate showed up. Christa easily answered the questions we had, and had numerous examples of what she had been through at her previous institution. She was hired not long after that, and a couple of months later on her first day, I saw her walking down the steps of the campus center during a crowded part of the day. She said "Hi Brianne." I remember only introducing myself as we all went around the table one day where she went through a gauntlet of interviews with numerous groups of staff, administration, and students. How the heck did she remember my name? I was impressed and amazed.

She immediately injected herself in the campus community, working her various groups into her agenda. The job required her to oversee the LGBTQ+ Affairs committee, and she became a co-chair. Our meetings remained fun, and became a bit more focused. She breathed such life into all of her programs, and was a teacher in all of the aspects of her position. It was clear the students quickly attached themselves to her, and I was amazed at her charisma, despite being someone not seeking the spotlight.

At this point in my development, I was making my way through so many changes and was beyond the shock factor of changing my name and pronouns, and was ready for the next portion of my journey. But what was the next part of the journey? I was moving through, and I was happy with myself every single day looking in the mirror, very appreciative of the campus community making the adjustments with my name and pronouns, and asking me about my journey and offering their best wishes and encouragement. But, what is next? What about all of the other trans people without this privilege? What about the black trans women that are being murdered at an alarming rate, increasing in deaths each year that goes by? What about kids that know something is going on with their sexuality and gender, but because of closed-minded parents and discriminatory laws cannot do anything about it? How do I figure myself out? And how do I bridge the gap between Jade and I within our relationship, in which she basically hates me at this point?

I was not aware of how much I would learn in the next couple of years, and how much I would be supported. I was amazed at how Christa could elevate all of these underrepresented groups on campus. She expertly mentored the students to conduct the various programs that had already been established, such as the "Identity Dialogues," where several students answer questions and explain their point of view on very difficult personal topics and various aspects of their identity as a part of a marginalized population. Other programs included "Spill the Tea," where student-led discussions about difficult topics that come up in society, such as inclusion of trans people in sports.

One Spill The Tea took place regarding this topic–trans people in sports–I was not asked to be on that. Someone else from our department was asked to talk about NCAA rules regarding trans people, and I was really insulted as a trans woman who participated in sports and is on female hormones and testosterone blockers, an experience I felt had a great deal to add about this topic, and the only out trans woman on campus at that. I felt my voice did matter. In a sensitive conversation with Christa I learned about tokenism, where the only person in a room is asked to speak for the entire group of underrepresented people, for the simple reason that they happen to belong in that group of underrepresented people. She talked me off of the ledge, and I realized she did not want to ask me to talk about this as a method to protect me from that feeling. Being someone that likes to talk about who I am, I had not realized the discomfort that others feel during this.

I also saw her in a vulnerable position, as an Asian woman during a time when then-president Donald Trump would blame the entire Covid pandemic on China and that his followers would blame the Asian community for the entire world being shut down, repeatedly referring to the Covid-19 virus as the "China Virus." It did not help that so many of his followers would believe his every word, and would then incite violence toward Asian people all over the country, causing fear and panic throughout the entire Asian community. This affected what seemed to be the majority of Asian people, causing more and more fear by the day. Christa, with her grace and brilliance, hosted a Facebook live event which eloquently laid out the history of hate and racism against the Asian community. I was holding back tears watching her pain as she described what she and people that look like her go through every day for their entire lives. I felt for her, and I also felt for my daughter Jade, who looks like Christa, yet I did not know hardly anything about Asians being referred to as the "model minority" or any of the hateful words that they are called on a regular basis. I felt like a total failure as a parent, a friend and an advocate, yet invigorated by learning about this.

Christa teamed up with Gretchel and another colleague, published an op-ed to address anti-Asian violence and Xenophobia, and once again, I learned more, and wanted to do more for this group of people, which happens to include one of my most favorite people in the world. This is something I never realized and have vowed to combat. I really found out what these women were made of.

That March, for International Women's Day, the person in Christa's position is usually in charge of arranging a keynote speaker to celebrate the day and inspire women to dream big and work hard for their goals. The Keynote speaker for March 8, 2021 was Rabbi Abby Stein, who was raised as a Jewish man in an Hasidic Jewish community, separated from her tight-knit community, transitioned into a woman and became a rabbi. She was such a truly inspiring human with an empowering story, and while I was amazed at this person's courageous story, I was blown away that someone would choose a trans woman to represent women in the first place, knowing there are countless successful and inspiring cis women all over that she could have invited. The exposure meant so much to me at that point, and I couldn't help but to think of the students that were exploring their gender with questions, and see this amazing person with such a special story and think that they could have some sort of hope. I also could not help but to think of how Christa went above and beyond to get someone who could touch so many different types of people. Attacks had recently taken place against Jewish places of worship, and the significance of a rabbi on International Women's Day was not lost. Christa is truly someone who is thinking big and trying to do the greatest good for the greatest number of people, and took a chance of upsetting some people who happened to think that this speaker represented just a segment of women, and only those of a certain religion. Christa demonstrated that the woman that happened to be trans and also happened to be Jewish did, indeed, represent all women, since Rabbi Abby Stein is, indeed, a woman. I am embarrassed to reveal that I did not catch on to this concept right away myself, but learned it clearly through this experience.

Among the greatest nights of the year that was defined by zoom meetings and webinars was the platform provided by Christa for me to host a panel discussion with three friends for Trans Day of Visibility. I celebrate this day every day, but this day was special, since we were able to tell our stories. I had three great guests as panelists, had over 45 viewers made up of friends, faculty, students, and coaches. I never felt so comfortable leading any discussion, and it was well received. It got back to me that one viewer mentioned to her husband that she thought I should be a talk show host. I never gave it any thought to even be able to speak in front of people, and I now have the ability and confidence to do just that, and I feel I now have a voice. I give myself visibility each day as I celebrate trans day of visibility and dress how I want to dress and present how I want to present. My confidence is on constant display, and a good chunk of this is from Christa's influence and the growth I was able to accomplish because of that. I have told Gretchel on many instances that Christa is by far her best hire, and I don't even know who else she has ever hired. I just know I am right on this one. Her job was to support, guide, and educate students and I may have been the biggest beneficiary of her brilliance.

31

FLOWERS, FOR ME? YOU SHOULDN'T HAVE

I HAD NEVER HAD FLOWERS GIVEN TO ME BEFORE. In fact, I rarely bought flowers for my wife. She loved flowers and all kinds of plants. I was intimidated growing any type of plants, I thought they were difficult to keep alive. She used to purchase plants and flowers for the backyard and front yard, and it was my job to plant them, and transplant them when she wanted a different arrangement. The plants inside in the several flower pots that were scattered all over the house were hers, since there were no holes to dig anywhere.

Flowers for special occasions? I did not see it, and could not understand purchasing flowers for a special occasion since it was an expensive gift for something that was going to die in a few days to a week. Flowers purchased as a gift were not a thing when I was growing up, and I just felt it was difficult for me to invest. My line of thinking in those days was why be the soft dude and get flowers for the girl? It was one way to keep up my persona to not be a softie, and to do things my own way.

For our first Valentine's Day together before we were married, I did not get flowers for Marian. She expected flowers but I didn't really have the money for them, and I was not sure what to do. I went shopping for something to get her, and realized that a stuffed animal would make a great gift, and would be more of a worthwhile investment since she could have this stuffed animal forever. This plan worked, until the next year, when she expected flowers, and I simply gave her a different stuffed animal. This continued throughout our 32-year relationship. The challenge for this was how to find a different animal for each year? It took a great deal of creativity, often different kinds of dogs.

Speaking of dogs, the other challenge was where to store all of these, and keep them away from the dogs? Especially when we had Baron, a large German Shepherd, who would chew up toys for fun, and even his robust toys were no match for Baron, let alone these soft stuffed animals. On the other hand, Bruno, our thirteen pound chiweenie, had other ideas for these gifts if he ever had the chance. These turned out to be his sex partners, and literally no stuffed animal was safe, species or gender. The dog was neutered, well allegedly anyway, and we were not veterinarians so this behavior did not add up to us. The bottom line was, we had a predator, and we needed to take caution of all of my valentine gifts or they would surely fall victim to his assaults.

All that said, I never got into the flower thing as a dude, and I really never thought of it as a woman. Two years into being out, I was coaching the Union Women's Club Ice Hockey team, and the last home game of the season was Senior day, where the seniors are honored by their teammates by a special introduction prior to the game, and presented with gifts following the game. This particular season, the players presented the seniors with gifts accompanied by a bouquet of flowers. Once the game was over and the players were still milling around the rink lobby talking and celebrating our win and the big day for the seniors, one of the players came to me with a bouquet of flowers in her hand and said, "Hey Brianne, these are for you."

Confused, I uttered, "Thank you? What are these for?"

I was wondering what was going on, and did not realize that these flowers were really for me, and why would anyone get me flowers?

"These are for you, thanks for all you do for us."

I later realized one of the seniors was not at the game, and these flowers would have been for her. I approached the player who gave them to me and mentioned to her and the other players that they really should give these flowers to her since she is the senior and they belong with her.

"No, really, these are for you; we want you to have these."

The double-agent spy in me figured out that I was not the intended recipient of the flowers originally, and they thought of the next best person to give them to. I felt bad for the girl that did not get them, and felt like I should be upset that they didn't think of me in the first place, and the overthinker in me finally realized a minute or so later that I should not have been presented flowers for senior day, since I was not a senior and had no business being honored. They did that since they had flowers and decided to give them to someone, and they chose me to thank me for my contributions to the program. I developed a bit of a lump in my throat.

I went back to that group and said, "I just wanted to thank you. I didn't mean to be difficult, and I really appreciate these. This is the first time I have ever received flowers from anyone, and I am touched. This is a great feeling."

Amidst a few awes, one of the girls said, "That's awesome, we are happy, getting flowers is a great feeling."

It is a great feeling. I have had it happen a couple of times since, and each time I feel a mix of joy to receive them, and guilt to have not ever given them. I never saw this, or realized how much this means to receive flowers. I learned a lot from this, and I regret not giving flowers more often, or even once, and will not make that mistake again. I cannot go back and give flowers to Marian, but moving forward I can and will do it for those that mean a lot to me. I would not have wanted them as a dude, but I have never or will ever take a gift of flowers for granted.

32

DESTINATION: COUGARVILLE

By this time, I was dressing as stereotypically feminine as I was able to, wearing dresses, heels, earrings, make up, but always feminine and a bit over the top at times. A lot of times, more and more as time went along. I seemed to wear things that were just a bit more than the situation calls for. There are few reasons for this and the main reason is because I could. Now I could wear what I wanted and hiding what I have longed to do for so long was no longer necessary.

Another reason was simply because I wanted to. I wanted, and still want to dress in bright colors. I had spent my life trying to figure out a style, for clothes, hair, and an overall look as a dude. I knew it had to be masculine in nature, often a golf shirt or an athletic jacket with some type of insignia of whatever team I am coaching or working for. No different than the majority of the other coaches, players, and administrators wear, particularly the men. I was somewhat conservative, no holes in jeans, baggy when baggy pants were in, normal relaxed fitting pants when that was in. I had the same five suits for the last twenty years or so. It was with my ties that I was able to somewhat set myself apart from anyone with flowery or bright, multi-colored ties. But for the most part, men have boring options when it comes time to dress up, and I know I had never enjoyed being involved with this.

Dressing up as a woman, on the other hand, is unique where the sky's the limit. All through my life, I have taken notes of various looks on women, both from those I knew and those I did not, and longed to have that opportunity to present myself like they did. Back when I started to dress as a woman at nights, or for an hour at a time here and there, I basically wore what I could find, and experimented with many different looks and styles. I would try to find things that could pair with many looks. The clothes, shoes, and accessories were always from thrift shops, for as cheap as I could get them, and always paid in cash. I could not afford a paper trail, thus I could never use a credit card. I felt good in whatever I was wearing at the time, just to have the chance to be there and act like a woman would act and feel what it feels like to be a woman, most importantly, what it would be like to be treated as a woman. My main goal was to find something that made me feel feminine, and that fit. I had never thought I would ever show my broad, manly shoulders, so any sleeveless garment was out. All I knew whether I liked what I was wearing or not, I felt natural, like I should be.

Once I came out, however, all bets were off. After decades of not being able to wear what I wanted to wear and what I would be comfortable wearing, I am finally free. Further, I had to present the way I was, as a woman with a fashion sense with loud colors just because it flat out makes me feel good. I looked in the mirror, and I saw a woman's body with a colorful dress on. I loved what I saw, and still do. In a short amount of time, I would only be seen in a skirt, a dress, or women's-cut shorts. I grew increasingly in touch with my love of pink, and the palette that stems from a regular pink through to hot pink, to any shade of purple, maroon, and royal and navy blue. Rarely would I wear orange and yellow, never green, and I stayed away from black unless it is an accent or if it is an amazing dress. I do NOT wear gray, and I mean, never. I spent a lifetime wearing gray and black, coaching shirts with logos on them, fitting in with what everyone else was wearing. I had a chance to stand out and express myself, and I intend to do just that. All of that reminds me of who I was, and I have no desire to revisit those looks or those feelings.

I feel normal when I dress this way with the loud colors, the louder the better, the way I feel I'm supposed to be. I am not going to lie, there were times that I thought this would wear off and I would slip back into jeans, sweats and coaching shirts, but that has never come close to happening throughout the five plus years as of this writing. Oftentimes, for the first fourteen months or so, I still would see "him" in the mirror. I would style my gray hair, attempting to grow it out into a more feminine look, but that would require long hair to cover the balding spots on my head, namely the back of my head where a natural yarmulke appeared to be forming, and the front on the sides where my hairline is receding. I knew wigs were always an option, but it was definitely not my first choice. I longed to look like the real, natural woman that I am. My hairdresser gave me a product to massage into my scalp that would stimulate hair growth from follicles that are still alive. While I could not tell, he said it was working a bit, but that I would always deal with that, and the trick would be to grow it so it is long enough to cover those thin or balding spots. I finally got the nerve, and enough money saved up from reffing hockey games, to get my hair done and colored a reddish blonde. Although my hair was getting longer and was looking rather good as a white/grayish color, I always loved the reddish-blonde color, and it was a bit like my natural hair color as a child. Based on my research, which consisted of trying on wigs of all colors, I decided to try it, as I thought I would look good as a blonde. I feel I was right, and have since added two inches of maroon color to the tips of my hair, which I never thought I would do. I absolutely love who I see in the mirror; I see a beautiful woman, and whether anyone else thinks so or not, I have the confidence that I can fit into any group or space, and I intend to occupy any space that I am in. Seeing myself in the mirror like this brought me joy, and still does.

There are other important reasons I dress the way I do, and they do not really involve me as much. It was important to me that when I came out, that I would do my best not to make others uncomfortable. I did not want anyone to have a doubt about how I am presenting, and how I would like to be addressed. I want friends, acquaintances, as well as strangers, to know they are looking at and talking to a woman, and save them the awkward or embarrassing moments trying to figure out who or what I am. I wanted it painfully obvious that I am a woman, and I am a ma'am, not even a consideration to call me sir. When they talk about me, I want them to automatically use she/her/hers pronouns, and not think twice.

Yes, I do want people to see me as a woman, and be treated as such. Truthfully, don't we all want to look as good as we can? Everyone can have different individual looks, body types, face shapes, and on and on. People have a different look they are going for, which is a very wide spectrum. But most of us try to do the best we can with what we have. For me, that means I want to pass as a woman as much as possible. I feel safe in that, if I walk into or out of some place and a transphobe happens to see me, they look the other way. In the region of the country in which I live and work, I have not had a problem, but I am not naïve enough to think that an ugly and/or dangerous confrontation will never happen to me. Before all of this, however, I just wanted to love the person I am looking at in the mirror. Once I could do that, it was easy to have the confidence to be in public and own who I am, to live my truth. Accomplishing this, in my estimation, will lower the probability that an ugly and/or dangerous confrontation will happen.

The other main reason I dress as feminine as possible is to show to others, those who may be hiding something similar to what I was hiding or questioning, that one can come from being a man for decades, and be able to come out and live my true life as a woman, and be proud of it. I have made myself more visible on campus which has been discussed, but a significant source of pride is when I am working as the event administrator at the Union College hockey games. It is important to me to be that role model, and this includes how I look, carry myself, and act. I cannot count the number of people that have approached me and told me that their son or brother became their daughter or sister, or their daughter or sister became their son or brother. This makes me feel great to hear this, to let them know that their loved one is not alone, and I always take the opportunity to thank them for being such a great support system to a trans person because we all do not have the support of our loved ones.

Of all of the comments I get about my looks, clothes, or anything else, it's the ones from parents that tell me that they think their child may be gender nonconforming in some way or another are among the most rewarding as a visible trans woman. I cannot express enough what Carolynn told me about me being a role model to others as a trans woman, and I take that seriously. I make sure these parents know that I speak from my perspective only and that everyone is different, and I make sure they know that they are the most amazing parents in the world for researching a very uncomfortable subject for a large portion of society.

I worked hard to take note of the typical differences in the behavioral and physical movement of transferring from a man to a woman, and did my best to adapt. Admittedly, some things took longer than others. The number of times people had to remind me to close my legs when I am sitting, well, I just cannot count those in the first few months. It remains the most difficult habit to break, along with not carrying the fingers closed in a bit of a fist while walking. I often curl my fingers in, as many men do, but women move in a flow rather, with their fingers extended. I learned this in voice lessons, of all places, and later at dance.

Speaking of hands, they are very important to me. Most trans women that I have known and talked to have something that triggers dysphoria. For some it is the hair, some the lips, the shoulders, feet, something that they just cannot stand to look at and drives them absolutely crazy. For me, it is my hands. I could be dressed to the nines, looking amazing, but one look at my man hands would put a damper on the whole thing. Cue the Seinfeld episode where Jerry was crazy about a girl he was seeing, until he looked at her hands which were larger and looked like a man's hands, and that killed the entire attraction. That is me. My nails need to be long. I realize acrylic ruins natural nails, but if I have them for the rest of my life, what's the difference? They elongate the fingers and make my hands much more feminine. Plus I have always loved the look. I need this, and am willing to referee hockey games or coach teams to make money to pay for them. Done Deal. Is it more difficult for me to do things with long nails? Not really, I simply get used to it and for the few things that are more difficult, it is more than worth it.

There are plenty of indicators to be able to clock a trans person, and one everyone seems to pick up on is voice. I can look as feminine as possible with the most outstanding outfit, but when I speak in a deep voice, one which I was never fond of anyway, it is the reddest flag you can have. I was fortunate to take a ten-week voice class for trans people at a local college, and it was a game-changer. The instructors were amazing, and they had graduate student interns helping us, giving us one on one attention. I was able to learn how to raise the tone of my voice and it was worth it. It is something I really have to work on, and some of the people told me that my voice is not a deep male voice. I begged to differ on this, and I worked on training my own since I would not return to classes due to work schedules and eventually the COVID-19 shutdown. I trained myself to raise the pitch of my voice and it usually works in public, although I often get lazy with it on the phone and get misgendered. For some reason it's taking a while to train my brain to keep my voice higher when answering a phone. It is frustrating, and I have been trying, but I seem to still struggle with it. Between the two, I would rather them misgender me on the phone.

Once in a while, someone would ask, "Oh yeah, Bri, another thing, what do you do about, ya know, down there? How do you hide, umm, it, umm them?"

My answer often is, "Oh, you must be talking about my genitals, how do I hide them? Yes, it is called tucking. I push everything under, so they are actually between the legs. The testosterone blockers shrink everything down there, and there are times I really do not need to tuck, depending on what I am wearing."

I have developed a sex drive, but much different than what I used to experience. I feel like all I want to do is hug, cuddle, and kiss. As a transbian, I only feel this libido when thinking about being with a woman. I did not begin to notice this until around my eighteenth month on hormones. I have yet to act on that; Marian made it clear she is not a lesbian, and I was not about to swerve outside of marriage. I can now tell very clearly that my sex drive and sexual feelings are not at all the same as they were before estrogen and the significantly decreased amount of testosterone running through my body.

I have been surprised at how little people ask me about my genitals. I had been warned that people would ask that all the time, but I seem to never get that question unless I am talking among trans people, as we all seem to have something in common. I'll tell you though, surgery is not in the plans; recovery is too long, it's expensive, and standing up to pee at times is still a perk I enjoy. Actually, I do not need to change my genitals to feel whole.

The look I am going for is "beautiful." I realize at my age, I may have only a little while left where I can look as attractive as I would have wanted to look throughout my life. Do I really want younger men to want to date me? Not really, I am a transbian, remember?

But if the younger guys, or anyone for that matter thinks I am attractive, that is just great, I am fine with that. I would say to people just as I was coming out, "I am fifty-four going on forty, with a fierce sense of fashion." I still have that dream of being a model, somehow, and that window is shrinking fast, so being a role model will suffice just fine. My new partner Laur is just fine with me just the way I am, and at this point, the age difference makes me a cougar, which I am great with.

If I needed a short answer as to why I wear the bright, loud colors is that for more than fifty years, I was wearing clothing I really did not want to wear, and now I don't have to do that. I can wear the clothes I want to wear and look how I want to look. I love the loud colors, particularly things that are different so I could somehow stand out in a crowd. Not only is it my hope that everyone can enjoy this freedom to wear what they want to wear and present how they want to present, but I realize I will not be stealth. Most people are and it is important to me that other trans people who are either out and nervous or not out can see someone that is living a great life and dressing how I feel the most comfortable. I am always thinking about my responsibilities as a role model.

33

PROUD

ONE OF THE MOST IMPORTANT WORDS TO ME AS AN LGBTQ+ community member is Pride. The Pride rallies and marches that take place each year internationally celebrate the gains made with individual self-acceptance, achievements, legal rights, and being proud of who we are as people. They usually take place in June to commemorate the Stonewall riots in New York City, when trans woman Marsha P. Johnson and other trans people led the patrons of the gay bar to stand up and fight against the police during a raid. This incident is a pivotal moment in the Pride movement and protests began the following year, and slowly evolved into parades all over the world to come together as a community and celebrate who we are.

What does pride mean to me? Well, that is simple, and complicated at the same time. I am tremendously happy and satisfied with who I am, who I've become, and the circumstances in which I have handled my coming out process. I love who I look at in the mirror, and feel pretty, feminine, and natural, just like who I thought I would look like throughout my life. I felt like this the day I came out to my wife and went to the beauty open house to learn about hair and makeup, despite how awkward I looked back then with my gray hair growing out of a man's haircut. I still feel that way every time I wake up and see myself in the mirror. I have the confidence to know I am prepared for this new life as an "out" trans woman. I also have the confidence to be able to speak up within a crowd, and to be able to say the right thing, or at least say what is on my mind. While I realize I may have to confront a hater at any time, I am confident about who I am despite who agrees or disagrees with me about speaking up. I have the confidence to help prepare others for their journey and to inform and educate others in order to make life more comfortable and inclusive for us. This is what describes the word pride to me.

Being proud to be trans throughout my journey is often seen differently to different people. For the allies, the people who are supportive, or at least open-minded, they tell me they feel inspired by the confidence and the willingness to speak the truth. Other people who do not believe we are real, or simply just don't like us, we can seem narcissistic. I heard that on occasion from inside my own house and within my extended family, and I often thought I did think too much about my looks, clothes, shoes (you definitely have me there), and my overall appearance. The way I am perceived and received by other people, both people I know and by strangers, is a huge part of what I pay attention to.

A case can be made that I was narcissistic, and I often thought that myself. One reason I feel a bit of guilt or at least uneasy feelings, is when my wife and best friend battled stage four cancer, with no encouragement from the medical community for a cure. She had been losing her hair, and color in her face ranges from pale and completely drained all the way to tomato red depending on the part of the chemo cycle she was on. When we first met, it was the 80's, and big hair was very much in style. I loved it, and I fell in love with her on sight. The big hair days are long gone, and she was consistently trying on different wigs and head coverings. Though she was having some fun with them, it was not was not exactly what anyone would want to go through. On top of feeling awful, sick, tired, and either nauseous or constipated on a good day, and absolutely in intolerable pain on other days, she was generally going through absolute hell. So when I show up with new hair, or worried about my acrylic nails falling off during a worldwide shutdown, or a new garment, or the worst yet, new shoes, this would not always go over all that well with her, and understandably so.

Herein lies the rub: I spent decades not feeling good about myself by looking at myself in the mirror and seeing something wrong with the reflection, and not knowing why. I did what I could about coming up with my own style, and looked as professional as I could, and did what I could to fit in. This is not to say that I was not proud of my accomplishments as a hockey player, a coach, an athletic administrator, a parent, and husband, or how I was able to make a positive impact on the lives of others, and my family. I was very proud to be a parent, and in the role I had. I was proud to be a father to our two children. There is one moment in time that illustrates this confusion.

In the spring of 2016, three years prior to coming out, I received a completely unexpected phone call from a member of the Kent State Athletic department, informing me that I was being inducted into the Kent State Athletic Hall of Fame. It was so unexpected, especially since I graduated in 1987, and although I was predominately a starting goalie, the program was discontinued in 1994 while I happened to be working there as an assistant coach. I was devastated at the time, along with being completely out of my mind pissed off. I not only lost a dream job at a school that I have loved since the day I stepped on the campus, but also lost a home in the city of Kent, Ohio. As a player, seeing the growth of the program from the time I was a freshman to my third year as an assistant coach was amazing. Having the program that I had so much pride in come to such an abrupt end was as demoralizing as half of my heart was ripped out of my body. They not only canceled hockey and Men's Gymnastics programs, there really was no real explanation given, and no opportunity to try to save it. They went so far as to never mention the sport in any of their information as if the sport never existed; it was a clean break. I had vowed that I would make a clean break and never again support this athletic department.

I did, however, have loyalty to my coaches that remained at the University and the area. Bill, who I worked for as his assistant coach, was offered a position directing the Ice Arena, and continued to run hockey schools there every summer. I was fortunate to be able to return each summer. Not only was his and his wife Sabrina's friendship important, but I could stay connected to the campus and the town. As time went along, there were a lot of changes, and it turns out that none of the same people were in the Kent State Athletic Administration anymore anymore, and they decided that hockey was once a varsity sport, and began to consider hockey players into the Hall of Fame. They had inducted one of my former teammates a few years prior to my induction class, so I figured they made their quota and there would never be a chance for me, if I even deserved it in the first place. To get this phone call was among the most proud moments of my life.

I had never given a lot of thought to this through the years, thinking that my playing career came and went and I was at peace with that. Receiving this phone call was an unbelievable feeling. I felt so good for my parents who supported me through all of the youth hockey and beyond, and provided me the opportunity to get to play college hockey. I was to be inducted in September 2016. I contacted Ernie, my first friend at Kent, goalie partner, and roommate, to let him know. Over time I realized how distant I must have been to many of my teammates, although I received a few heartfelt congratulatory emails, they were few and far between. I was honored that the coach that recruited me and made it all possible, Don Lumley, and his wife were there, along with my parents and brothers. Unfortunately, Marian could not make it through the nine hour drive while dealing with her chemo treatments from her first diagnosis, so I made the drive to Kent with Alex.

I remember vividly the empty feeling I had during this weekend. One was being nervous about making a speech in front of a crowded ballroom, always wondering how long it would take, knowing that I tend to ramble at that point in my life. I also had a difficult time with having such a validation without Marian there to celebrate with, and knowing how lousy she was feeling and how scary her situation was made my whole experience feel empty. I was not feeling like myself. The increasing confusion within the vault inside my brain, the increasing confusion about where I might have been headed, were really starting to peak. While I did not feel like myself, I was not sure if it was because Marian could not be with me to share in such a huge day, or if it was something else. I honestly wondered if it had something to do with the impending discussion I would eventually have with my parents and brothers who were there for the event, but if it wasn't that, it definitely was the secret. I really thought this speech I was giving was going to be given by the persona that was reserved, not quite confident or comfortable, the shy person that was acting as if I was, in fact, a person that would not think about being mushy in a speech, let alone show a lot of passion. I could usually call it up while I was coaching, since I knew what I was doing, but in these times, I didn't quite know what I was doing. I was confused and literally felt as if I was in between lives. I wanted so badly to have a confident, vibrant, enthusiastic, sincere, and honest person up there to do the talking, the person I was beginning to think that Brianne somehow would become. I was not sure I was proud of the person that gave that speech; I felt flawed, defective in some way even though the very people that were there to support me were the people whose opinion mattered most to me. I felt empty. Usually if I get nervous before a presentation, I feel relieved afterward. This time, I was not relieved. Something has to happen at some point, but how? After all of the time I have tried to find a way out of the vault, it kept feeling like it was closing in.

When that weekend was said and done, I felt like I had just been through the most emotional weekend I had ever been on. Looking back on that, I was tremendously proud of the accomplishment, and that people would think enough of me to induct me into their Hall of Fame, and I felt like I was trying to feel like I was on top of the world. At least I should have felt that way, but I was disappointed that I felt so empty and stalled inside of my head that I could not have more positive feelings about myself while going through a once in a lifetime experience.

It was sort of a once in a lifetime experience. Fast forward to November of 2019, five months after my official public outing, when the President of the Vianney High School Hockey Club, my high school that I played for two seasons, called me out of the blue. I had known him since my very first year playing hockey at age seven, and throughout our playing days, as he was a year older than I was, and I really was not on his team again until high school. He was always setting up the Alumni games each year within the Christmas holiday, of which I attended one, due to this being in St. Louis and I don't always get back there during that time.

This time he told me I was being inducted to the high school program's Hall of Fame. I was really shocked, as I said, I played only two seasons, and one of them I was a backup goalie. We had a conversation about it, but this time, I disclosed my transition, let him know my new name, and asked him how it should be handled. This was going to be on a nice plaque that they would send, but also on a banner hanging at the rink that I grew up playing in. This was a big decision. I suggested that I use the name Brianne "Dead-name" Brinker. I felt it was fair that I used my deadname since that was my name when I was competing and earning that honor. He felt the same way. My mother was more than upset when she saw a picture of the plaque on Facebook, but I felt this was the most fair way to do it, fair to the program, to my parents, and to me. She thought I was changing history due to something that I could not remember. I could not make the event to give any type of speech, but I wrote a letter to be read to the group. I was ready for this one, even though this was more of a surprise than the last one. I felt proud of who I was, and was more proud of who I used to be than when I was actually that person.

Somehow, I am more than willing to be myself, and to show myself to everyone. I am comfortable to be in front of groups, and can speak within and to a crowd. I have a lot to say about my community and myself, and I intend to say what I need to say to lift up my community and stand up to the haters and even educate whoever needs it. I am proud to be able to do that, and if that makes me narcissistic, then I'm guilty as charged.

34

MARIAN'S TRANSITION

FOR MARIAN, THINGS TURNED FOR THE WORST TOWARD the end of March 2021. Her scan revealed that the chemo treatments were no longer working, and a very important decision had to be made. The disease had spread, possibly to the brain, since the lymph system can transport it to all parts of the body. She hadn't been able to drive for over a couple of years at this point, and her mind was starting to go, her memory was not anything like she used to be–the family historian, the side-splitting storyteller, the brilliant writer of our family milestones was no longer able to recall things she used to. She was losing her superpower, and she knew it. She realized it before any of us did, and she did not like it, not one bit.

She hated it, as she had begun to take on uncomfortable tasks like looking at the life insurance policy, showing me her method of paying bills online and other affairs to get in order. She had been preparing me for a while for this, and at the same time, preparing herself, the kids, and others. The part involving my preparation was welcomed, as I had already taken over the bills, and we reviewed any money information, such as retirement, life insurance, Roth IRA's, and the like. She did not want to worry about it anymore, she can wipe her hands clean of all of it. My part was to learn about these items, and most importantly, show her that I had a handle on this so she would not have to worry once she was no longer able to handle any of it. She could literally relax, and finish things in peace. I felt empowered a bit, and had control of what was needed for a few months into the future.

Preparing herself, well, that was a different story. But she knew it was time. She was frustrated, but when the palliative care nurses, who we both loved to visit with, suggested that hospice could give her a more comfortable existence and could do more than they themselves could, she knew what the decision had to be. We still went home to talk about it, because that is what we always did when there was a life-changing situation, such as buying a car, taking a new job, going through the various methods of becoming parents. This decision was the easiest for her. She knew hospice would be the way she had to go. She courageously chose hospice, as if she was now ready to cross over to whatever awaited her, if anything at all.

She was not quite that ready. It was her goal to be able to see both of the kids graduate high school, which happened one month apart. Jade in May, at Canterbury School in Connecticut, over two hours away from the house. She looked amazing that day, and was excited to take her pictures, which she loves to do, capturing the joy of the day. Her photos were amazing, as usual, and she was radiant the entire day, as she somehow had the energy to soak up the festivities and help load the vehicle with Jade's belongings to travel back home. Her pride in Jade was immeasurable, and she used up every ounce of energy she had to enjoy every minute of it. My emotions were running wild seeing her rally to celebrate Jade, and enjoy everything that went with it. I was so proud of both of them as I stayed in the background watching them soak it all up.

What was telling about her transformation was the decline by the time she was able to attend Alex's graduation ceremony a month later in late June at Schenectady High School, located eight doors down from our house, and a walk around to the football field in the back of the building. She was excited for this, and really proud of Alex, and in turn, of herself. She spent every year of Alex's life tirelessly working on his habits and advocating for his schooling and services. So much of his success was in such a large way a result of her loving attention and efforts. He graduated with academic honors and was an athlete on the bowling team for three years and a diver on the swimming and diving team, thus totalling athletic endeavors for four years allowing him to wear a stole to commemorate honor students and athletes, neither of which we would have dreamed of from the beginning.

Again, her pride was palpable, but her energy level was decreasing with each passing week. It took a while to walk up to the high school, which was the shortest possible walk we could have. She made it there and was able to understand what was going on. She was able to witness one more time the special admiration Alex had for his teachers at the school. This would be the final major event that she had to look forward to, and it showed. Our anniversary was coming up, but that was not as important to her as the maturation and the success of her kids. We were able to have friends visit, both local and from out of town. Several high school friends drove to town to visit basically to say goodbye, and we had a bunch of local friends that would come over to the house to spend time with her, and watch her while I was able to either go down to campus for work or to escape with a bike ride.

The bike rides ended as August came, as did the time that Jessica, Susan, and Laura would spend with her. During this time, she would try to get out of her bed, and squeeze between the table tray and the bars to try to get out, but she could no longer walk by herself by the end of August. Visitors would no longer be able to come as she would not want to be seen in the state of decline that she was at. I could not have stayed sane and kept my head into the game without the constant time and effort from Lisa and Kristine, her close friends we knew for many years from the church. They came over a couple of times each week, and gave me a break from the constant watch.

She had already been moved downstairs to a hospital bed provided by hospice, along with plenty of other apparatus that we may later need: a cane, walker, a wheelchair, commode for the room, and other supplies. The table next to her bed was full of pill bottles, lotions, and the familiar gatorade bottles, which was her go-to drink for the five and a half years she was dealing with chemo treatments. She would send me to one of two of the locally owned coffee shops in town to get either a bubble tea and a scone, or a chai latte with a quiche. Throughout the summer she settled into a habit of writing a letter each day to someone, copying the poem of the day that she retrieved off of a website by hand, and color a picture from one of her several coloring books to illustrate the poem she had just read and copied. She made every attempt to keep her hands moving and her mind operating as much as possible, as she was realizing she would need to use her motor skills or lose them. As time moved along through July into August, she was no longer able to concentrate on reading the countless books she had bought for this experience, and her time-passing hobby turned into strictly coloring and writing letters. Her coloring in April and May was very particular with proper colors, all in the lines, each space with its own color. She easily had more than 200 different markers, and she needed to take every single one of them wherever she went to color, along with her binder of colored pages, which by July was getting quite extensive. She would bring a handful of cups stuffed with markers of the same color, and place it on the table. This process took place whether we were sitting outside, on the couch, or in her bed. These items made her feel safe, and worthwhile, like what she was doing still mattered. She was proud of these. As the calendar moved into August and her speech was getting more and more difficult to understand, her pictures were getting more and more difficult to figure out. We were witnessing such a decline, with me now administering her meds (mainly morphine for pain control) around the clock. I slept in the recliner just outside the door in the living room, the one we bought early on in our marriage, so I could be available at any time and so I could see her as soon as I woke up. It is where I had slept since her journey began so I would not wake her up and disrupt her already difficult sleeping patterns.

By the last week of August, the Hospice nurse suggested I keep a constant eye on her as she could go at any time. This was around the time she started to reject food and water. One hospice nurse after the other had warned that her time could be any day, and it could happen at any time, which meant a 24-hour watch. Around that time, something had dawned on me, that I was ready for what was about to happen. I was ready with funeral plans, keeping our families posted about her progression toward her future surroundings. While I was still trying to keep up with work on campus to take my mind off of the inevitable, I realized that I was and had been mourning the process, and I was sharply aware that I was very comfortable with myself as Brianne, and that my transformation was, indeed, necessary for me to be there to assist her with her transformation. My escape from the vault never seemed so critical as it did in these September days, waiting for her to end her journey and begin what she believed would be her new one, whatever that would be. Day after day, pill after pill, we were wondering when this would happen since Hospice warned us.

Wednesday morning, October 6, was a day I cannot forget, as that is the day it really hit me in the face that her last breaths were upon us. I really took time to notice just how dry her mouth was from not eating or drinking anything in the last two and a half weeks. I took my time that morning, cleaned her teeth and her mouth extra well, and gave her a long full body massage. This was a particularly difficult day, perhaps the most difficult day of this journey. The destruction to such an incredible human life became very evident, and for the first time I had a very difficult time. I had a lump in my throat the entire day, trying to make her more comfortable, and having little to no indication if I was successful. In those moments, I realized something I had thought for a long time and I was convinced of; if there is a god, a celestial being that loves all of us and has a plan for us all, that if the plan is to inflict a devastating, incurable disease into someone and not take it away, making a person hang on for 21 straight days since her last bite of food, and eighteen days since her last swallow of water, that is not a god that the churches boast about, and if it is, it is not one I care to be involved with. That the dots could not be connected to any sensible logic was crystal clear evidence to me, and I became an unapologetic atheist that morning.

October 8, 2021, the nurse that came in to clean her up and check, and said if we were to contact family, now is the time. I was ready for this. I contacted her family and arranged a zoom call with her the next day from her room, so they could tell her it was ok to move on. I knew she heard their voices and could understand clearly, she even made facial gestures to the camera. They did not want to see her in this state. I arranged for my family to do the same later in the day on Saturday night. I was at peace that this was done, and was ready for this to go down.

At 4:00am on Sunday morning, I woke up at the usual time to give her the morphine, and she settled down and went back to sleep. I somehow went back to sleep in the chair. At 7:50am I woke to the sounds of Marian grunting louder than she had grunted in a long time, and louder than she had groaned from the pain. After living with her for 32 years, I knew just what she was saying to me, "Hey! HEY! Get your ass in here so I can say goodbye, NOW!"

I came over, knowing this was it. I gave her more morphine for any pain that she may have, so she can expire as comfortably as possible. I was tired as could be but never more in the moment. I held her hand, gave her several kisses on the head and cheeks, and told her, "It's OK, I've got this." I still think she actually knew that was bullshit, but she knew it was time. We continued to hold hands, and within twenty minutes, at 8:10am, she coughed, grunted louder than usual, then seemed to take her last breath. I continued to hold her hand and rub her arms and legs, checking her nose to detect breath. Another ten minutes made up the most peaceful and solemn moments I have ever experienced. I realized the privilege I had to be able to be there for my best friend and the person that was with me for so many of my dark moments during her last moment. I had read in Hospice literature and in other places not to be in a hurry to contact Hospice immediately after breath stops. They were not going to revive her, and it was a peaceful moment for us to share. I was honored to be there, the first time I was with a dead human being.

At 8:25am I went upstairs and woke Alex up and asked him if he wanted to say goodbye to her body before the funeral home came to get her, and he did. He sat staring at her while I contacted Hospice, which triggered someone to come over to pronounce her dead. Neither of us were crying at the time. The Hospice nurse was there by 9:15am to pronounce her and get her ready to go. The funeral home was there at 10:15am after Alex had gone to church, so neither of the kids had to watch her get carried out of the house. The body was gone by 10:35am, and both of the kids were able to say goodbye in the ways that made them comfortable.

One memorable moment: Marian's little dog and companion, Bruno, had jumped up and laid next to Marian the entire time we were in there, just as he had done for the last several years. The Hospice nurse could not have been nicer as we chatted while she began to get her ready. I realized I did not want to see her being prepared to be put in a large bag to get her out of there and I went to the back yard and threw tennis balls to Baron, our German Shepard. After fifteen minutes, I walked back into the room to see Bruno with his front paws on her chest, licking her face like crazy, with Marian's left arm on top of Bruno as if she was petting him.

Immediately spooked, I blurted out "Oh My God, What The Fu…?"

Did I jump the gun and miss something, is she still going? Her arm was not moving on its own before. I looked at the nurse, and she gave a cute little grin, saying she thought the little dog was so cute licking her face, and that she placed Marian's arm on Bruno. She was so right. It was precious. Marian would never allow that to happen if she could help it, but at this point, I am positive it was perfectly fine with her, as it appeared he was trying to wake her up. I tried to get a video of this, but could not get my phone to work at that moment, and he stopped just as I finally got the video working. Just as well, that was so cute but if there is no picture, there is no way anyone would see her in that situation.

35

THE FINAL DESCENT: NOW WHAT?

So now what? What do I do now? I had not thought about how I felt, just that I was tired, but somehow energized at the same time. I felt a bit lighter that she wasn't hanging on depending on heavy duty drugs to keep her comfortable. I recalled that she had said a couple of times throughout the journey that she would not fight just to live a couple more miserable days, and that she saw no point putting the family through that. Although she wound up hanging on and was clearly fighting until the last day, I realized she was done with the battle and that was a positive thing.

I texted all family members that I needed to contact, and I prepared a Facebook post to be posted once enough of the family members acknowledged my text. Then I went to downtown Schenectady to the farmers market to walk around. I felt a bit relieved, a bit sad, and mostly numb all at the same time. I was thinking about what I would say at the funeral, how it would look, how I would announce it, and decided it should be in two weekends to give people from out of town a chance to make plans to travel. But, truthfully, I needed a week to get to work, catch up a bit, and take my mind off of the ordeal for a bit, be as normal as possible, then take a week off and plan the funeral and all things that go with it. I needed a break, and that break would come in the form of getting back into my normal routine.

When I came back home, I just started to clean up some of the sheets and strip the bed. I put everything in the washing machine, and began to craft an email to family to reveal funeral plans, and within this to let everyone know that it was our family's time to mourn, that we would love for them to be there, and that they were welcome with the stipulation that they are not critical of the process of the care I gave for Marian (which some of them had been without any knowledge), and that they respect the boundaries of using proper pronouns and names for everyone. This invitation was not sent to everyone in Marian's family due to their problematic behavior during the process, and their unwillingness to be nice. I knew the word would spread, and this was just as much for us as a family, and me as the primary caregiver and long time spouse. I am sure I was accused of being selfish and egotistical, but I wanted and needed peace there during that time.

While getting the funeral plans together, part of me was thinking about what was going to happen with people that have not bought into my transition, and I was determined to not let it bother me, and be who I was. Who I was at the time was a confident, proud, and visible trans woman with boundaries. Not knowing what to expect, I was ready to put a funeral together to respect and honor the tremendous person and her influential life. I thought daily about what I would say to eulogize her, and had it ready on paper, although when the time came to do it I did not need the written script, nor did I read from it. I was in the moment, it was time to deliver, and it turned out very well.

It was great to see Marian's high school and childhood friends travel to be here to honor her, along with my two nieces from my side of the family, who took time off of school, one of them missing a college soccer game to be there. Among the notable parts of the funeral weekend for me took place at dinner on Friday night. The night before the funeral, my mother complimented me on my new boots that I had bought that day while I was waiting for her to get ready. I bought two pairs, the same model but different colors. Doing that made me feel very comfortable being myself and not worrying about people bothered by the fact that I was once of a different gender, or that I was a sinner, or whatever else one could come up with from a devoted Catholic and Republican.

The gender euphoria really came the following night at dinner, after the day featuring the wake, the funeral, the luncheon following the funeral provided by Marian's brother and time spent at their AirBnb with her side of the family. Finally dinner with my family and two nieces. I still had my Calvin Klein color block dress that I felt absolutely stunning in, and my mother came up to me while we were waiting for a table and said, "I meant to tell you, I love your dress, and you look very pretty in it."

That comment made my entire weekend after two and a half years of not appreciating me and who I was. Although I had more confidence that I never knew I could have, this was the most euphoric comment I could have asked for. The person I respected more than anyone, despite clashing politically in every way, validated my existence. I am ready for anything else that could possibly come my way.

36

JOY TO MY WORLD: TEAM TRANS

DURING THE SUMMER, TEAM TRANS, THE ADULT, ALL trans and non-binary hockey team, was putting out information about their Friendship Series to be played in Madison, WI on the weekend of November 19-21, 2021. By August, it was becoming clear that Marian would not make it past September, or possibly early October. I was intrigued, even though I had not played a bit of hockey in at least twelve years. I had to think about this situation, and seriously consider being able to attend this. Was I mentally able to do this? How would grieving go? How upset at myself would I be if I missed this opportunity to play hockey on a team with all trans people on it?

A colleague and friend from campus had spent time with me once a week on Zoom throughout July and August while Marian was in Hospice, once Marian's decline was beginning to accelerate. My friend had a similar experience with her husband who went through a very long illness a couple of years prior. It was so therapeutic to be able to speak with her, and she was genuinely gracious with her time sharing her experiences. Almost everything she told me about her experience happened with our situation, either it had already happened, or happened within a week of our discussion. Among her experiences that stuck out to me was when her husband passed, she went out of town for a few days just to get away, unwind, and process the information. I realize a lot of people get their funeral arrangements right away, but I knew early on I would not be able to do it that early, despite how much preparation I have emotionally and with arrangements.

The day to day care that went into it was exhausting physically, mentally, and emotionally, and I was really feeling like my friend had given me a terrific idea. This particular weekend with Team Trans happened to fall on the weekend of finals for the Union College students, which means we would have no athletic events scheduled. Team Trans was started a year prior to this, in 2018, when a couple of trans hockey players had a connection to Boston Pride Hockey, an adult queer hockey organization that agreed to support this idea to play hockey games against the group of trans hockey players. I became aware of this endeavor through Facebook, but I knew I did not have the time and money to participate, let alone I was taking care of my sick wife. Now that I am newly single and an out trans woman, in 2021, I took advantage of the one weekend of the year that I could get away and not miss any events at work. I had been away from the office, and not able to fulfill all of my responsibilities to the fullest extent already. I did not want to miss anything else since the department was so understanding of my situation. And this was a weekend full of trans people playing hockey. What could be better than a combination of my two favorite ways to spend my time? Hockey and meeting and talking to trans people that have that common love, what could be better? I emailed Mason, who I had met while he was living here, and playing with the Albany Bombers, an all queer hockey team, to tell him I ordered a jersey, and would arrange payment later. I chose number 1, which was my college hockey number and a number traditionally used by goalies, and even though I would not play goal again, I chose that number that I had always cherished since being a little kid. During the month between the funeral and the Friendship Series, I was getting downright excited to get going. I was nervous that I would be out of shape, but I had little time to do anything about that. I was beyond excited with anticipation for this, and I began to worry that this experience could not live up to my lofty expectations of a flawless, perfect, life-changing event. I did not want to be let down, but I was going to drive out to Madison, around a fourteen hour drive if I went directly.

The trip could not have been better. It all started with my drive out at the beginning of my eight day excursion. I drove to Olean to check in with my father-in-law, who was struggling through his own battle with cancer, along with the death of his beloved daughter. It was nice to share a sub from my favorite sub shop in the world, and likely the smallest shop in the world, On The Side, in Olean, NY. I'm guessing this place might be eight feet wide and long enough for three booths situated back to back from door to counter. I cannot remember a better sub, and I return there to On the Side every time I am in town.

I continued on to outside Akron, OH, where I would stay with Ernie, my college roommate, goalie partner and best friend. I was able to spend time with him and his wife, Clarissa, and stayed at their place for the night. It was comforting to be among friends that have known me for most of my life and cared for me unconditionally. I continued on to Columbus, OH to visit another college friend, and on to Cincinnati, where I am not sure I ever laughed so much with my first recruit as a coach at the University of Findlay, Manda. Being able to talk to her about many things was amazing, and we had so much fun window shopping near the University of Cincinnati. We had become close through the recent years and I am grateful to be able to reconnect with someone I care so much about.

On to Madison, with a stop in Chicago to visit my friend from college, Jeanne, who I had not seen in over thirty years, but someone I always admired and looked up to. We were both athletes in the same years at Kent, and I was amazed at her confidence and leadership ability, and mostly her fun-loving demeanor. It was amazing to sit with her and see how well she was doing, already retired with three grown kids, of whom she is immensely proud. I then continued on to Madison to check into my hotel and to visit with Josh, my good friend and one-time assistant coach at Findlay. It was great catching up with his new career in the airline industry.

After dinner, it was time to check in at the home of Avery and Mason, prior to our 10:00 pm practice that Friday night. I had looked forward to this weekend for so long, and even though I had been loaded with confidence and self-assurance in who I am, I was anxious, excited, and a bit nervous. I knocked on the door, and heard a couple of people yell, "Come in." I opened the door and immediately hit a guy in the butt with the door, causing him to half fall down over the boxes next to the door. I said I am sorry to one of the most attractive men I had ever met, and it took me a bit to realize he was trans. Even though this was a trans hockey team, and he had his jersey and socks in his hand, I still thought he was cis. He was extremely friendly after the awkward introduction. From Nova Scotia, Canada, as a former national level ringette player in his childhood as a Canadian, he turned out to be our best skater and player that weekend and a really friendly and personable guy.

I was given a t-shirt to commemorate the Friendship Series, and then they gave me my uniform jersey and socks. I felt like I did when I received my first hockey jersey as a little kid, which was at the time a green jersey and socks with South Side Machine printed on the front of it, and a Minnesota North Stars logo in the middle of the writing. I do not remember my number on my first jersey, but that was the last year I played any position besides goalie until well after college. I was number one the next year and for the next several years. Seeing my first college jersey hanging up in my locker with my name on the back and the number one on it was a thrill, a dream fulfilled. I have had so many jerseys along the way and was proud of every team I played for through the years, but none more so than the Kent State jersey.

But this half light blue and dark pink Team Trans jersey was so special. So special. I could not wait to get to the rink, get dressed, and put this uniform on. I felt like a little kid again, on my first team, not knowing anyone, but being so excited to be there. The feeling also resembled my first college game, not knowing exactly what to expect, but knowing I could believe in myself, and that was enough to carry me through and succeed, and know that all of the effort and work has paid off. But, I felt jitters like I had not felt in a long time. I was the first one to the rink and to walk into the lobby, followed by a tall trans girl with blue hair and the largest smile on her face named Kriona. She was such a friendly and positive person who lives locally, and with her was Brennan, a shorter trans guy, who lived in my area and plays for the Albany Bombers. So, we chatted until others showed up and the locker rooms were available, then went to get our gear on and get ready.

I have been in many locker rooms through the years, of all levels of hockey, both as a player and a coach. But this locker room experience was an experience unlike any other. Everyone walking into this room was a gender nonconforming individual who played hockey. Every player was just as friendly as the next. I needed a couple of helmet screws for my helmet, and Petey, a really cool non-binary individual, had a spare kit with all kinds of snaps, screws, and even a screwdriver, and was more than willing to help. I sat next to K8, as they called themself, and they showed me the team lists, which showed me on the advanced team, which is the top team, and as I was looking around, there was a lot of people a lot younger than I was (in fact, at age 56 everyone there was younger than I was). I introduced myself to as many people as I could, and tried to remember names and pronouns. I came to find out there were players from all over the country, and Canada, and even Daniel, who is a founding member of Team Trans who flew in from Tokyo, Japan, where he worked at the American embassy. Daniel is a gentleman in every way, as nice as anyone I have ever met. It was a room where all sorts of topics were talked about, including me asking if any of the trans women had an extra estradiol patch since I forgot to bring an extra one, sparking a conversation about which other methods the trans women get their estrogen, which to that point I had never heard discussed in a hockey locker room before, or anywhere with a group that was not a support group.

For the oldest player out of all 47 there, the workout was simply grueling, absolutely painful. I was so out of shape, and the coach was having us do skating drills, and a bunch of them. I was not the worst skater there, and thankfully, there were others that were exhausted, as well. After each drill repetition, we returned to the lines and I found someone else to introduce myself to, find out where they are from, their pronouns, and I could not meet enough people. I was on a mission to meet every person on the ice, however impossible that was. That part was the part that was so energizing, it helped us through every single drill on the ice. As tired and sore as my legs were getting, the more energized I became as I was meeting more and more trans people that were as excited as I was to be there.

Practice ended, and we took a picture of the entire group, all 47 of us. It was amazing to see all of this. I remember the buzz of everyone talking about how they have never seen this many trans people in the same place at the same time, and on the ice. People that are just like we are, with similar stories, with struggles and triumphs, with fears and strengths, and everyone gaining affirmation by the minute. I was thinking to myself how I had never felt so much positivity and excitement in one place, and after practice and the team picture I realized I needed to go to the locker room and get my phone to get pictures of those I had met so far. The smiles were absolutely infectious, before we even played a single game and had a drink with each other. I started to realize along with everyone else, that this was something very special, some-thing that is more unique than any of us has ever experienced before, and this wave of positivity and joy was unstoppable.

I was among the last to leave the locker room once we finally left the ice. Many players seemed to take their time leaving, trying to savor the experience. Perhaps it had something to do being exhausted, but we were honestly enjoying each other's company. I was not in a hurry to leave, as I knew I would not fall asleep for a long while due to the adrenaline still racing through my system. During this time, Daniel said something I had never heard in a locker room before and will never forget. While walking out the door after practice, he said to the room, "Alright see you all tomor-row, I love you all." I'll never forget that. Saying I love you is some-thing I had been saying to many people through the past couple of years, and I like to be able to say it to people I love. I did not grow up saying that as it was not said in our house, especially by any of the four male-identified members of our household. To hear such a well-spoken man say that to a bunch of people who he may not know and has just met, but knows who we are and what we have been through, was as impactful as anything I heard all weekend, or ever. At that point, I realized I could say that to a group, because I loved hearing it, and I can mean it.

That night, at the hotel, I could not help but to put on my jersey again, and take selfies of it in the mirror. I have really loved looking at myself in the mirror for the previous two and a half years, and I had not ever looked at myself modeling this amazing jersey. I could not believe it. I am not a person that wears my jersey around, but I did not want to take this off. So I slept in it, if you can call it that. I was all over that bed, trying to sleep but trying to savor the feeling I had from this night for as long as possible. I remember looking at the clock at some point and it said 4:10 am. I simply could not sleep because the night had such an impact. I could not imagine the next day being able to top the experience we just went through. I wanted to get to the rink around 12:30 pm for the first game, after I had breakfast with my friend Sarah, who I had not seen in a while and lives in the area. I could not stop talking about the night before. She was intrigued and excited, and actually came to watch me play on Sunday.

The next two days may not have exceeded the first impactful night, but they were every bit as exhilarating. There were three games being played each day, with each of our three teams playing one of the teams from the Madison Gay Hockey Association, a very impressive league of queer hockey players with many teams competing at three different levels. I recorded the two games before ours to webstream to the app twitch, so families and friends could see the games from their hometowns. I spent this time with Michelle, another trans woman on my team and a lovely, intelligent and fun person. We spent the day getting to know each other, and we easily became friends. Our teams could not have had a better weekend, with our teams sweeping the series, but most of all, being together. Playing hockey again was fun, but oh my freaking god, I was so out of shape. My shifts were by far shorter than anyone else's. I am not one to stay out on a shift if I am tired when someone else is on the bench and is more fresh and can do a better job. It was so fun just to be there on a team again.

The amazing part of this entire experience was, while the hockey was fun, the camaraderie off the ice was transformative. We had a social gathering on Saturday night that most of the group attended. We were able to mingle and spend time with several different people, getting to know them, their backgrounds, and for some, their journeys. I was making sure I got selfies with as many people that I talked to, as I wanted to savor these moments and these budding friendships. Again, on brand, I was among the last to leave, not wanting anything to end. I may have got more sleep that night, but the morning arrived early and before I knew it, we were back at the rink, either playing or watching the other teams play.

It took awhile to get to the locker room when the second game was over on Sunday. We shook hands with the opponent, took more team pictures, more selfies, and just skating around--none of us wanted to get off of the ice, no one wanted it to end. I remember a teammate skating by me saying "I just don't want to leave." I felt the same way, a similar feeling to the one I had after my final college hockey game, which was at Notre Dame. I did not want to leave. We won both of our games by the way.

In the locker room once they finally kicked us off the ice, no one seemed to be in a hurry to get out of the locker room, even though many of us had long trips ahead of us. There were selfies and hugs all over the place, and I did not cheat myself on this. I made a point to visit with everyone in the room to let them know how much I enjoyed being with them, and wanted to stay in touch. Daniel, as the president of the Team Trans Board, said some words to the group, as did Mason and others. Mason was one of the primary organizers of the event and had a couple of special game pucks to give out. One of them happened to me. One of the most sincere people I know, he said some things to the group that "the one person he was happy to see there was Brianne, since it was touch and go with what she had been through, and I had been a bit non-committal whether I could make it until a bit later in the process." I accepted the puck and added a quip that was something along the lines that I deserved that puck since I added "age and penalty minutes to the success," which are not exactly beneficial to help a team win. I mainly used the opportunity to let the group know how much I appreciated them, and that I thoroughly enjoyed the special experience. I remember sharing that I had a lot of accomplishments in hockey, playing and coaching, including being in my college's Hall of Fame, but of all of these, this was the most special weekend that I had in hockey, because of what we represented. I was sad the weekend had to end.

Instead of leaving right after I was dressed and out of the room, I joined a group of people from our program for lunch. I then jumped in the car with my drinks and snacks for the ride back home, hoping to make it five to six hours to Toledo that night to stop and sleep. I was still wound up driving back through Chicago late on a Sunday afternoon, and started to become tired in mid-Indiana around 11:00 pm or so. Just for the heck of it, I decided to text Michelle to let her know where I was staying on the off chance that she stopped in the same area, maybe the same exit with hotels located there, that maybe, just maybe, she wanted to get a drink.

My text to her was, "Just in case you are at the same exit, I am at the Motel 6 in Toledo, and if you are nearby and awake, would you want to grab a drink?"

Her text replied, "What, Omg, I'm at the Motel 6 in Toledo too! What a small world. Wanna come down to my room for a drink? I'm in room 131."

So we sat around and drank a couple of her souvenir IPAs from Wisconsin, and we talked about the weekend, the people, the feelings, and each other, getting to know one another. I knew she was into so many things, and she even brought her guitar that her brother hand-made and played and sang a couple of songs. What an incredible way to extend the beautiful weekend, not to mention losing more sleep as we were both getting up early to travel back home. I had three more stops to make, one with Mike, a good friend from when we lived in Findlay. I then drove to Kent, picked up some food and stopped in to see Coach Lumley and his wife Elaine. It was great to see both of them, two people who decades prior changed the course of my life. We talked for a couple of hours, catching up on the families and I had a chance to verbalize how much they meant to me and that I loved them. I really wanted to tell them both how much they meant to me.

I then headed for Ellicottville, NY where I stayed with Katie and Maria, sisters that were lifelong friends with Marian. Maria, the person who introduced us and Marian were literally born four days apart, and their families had been friends, so they literally grew up together. They were nice enough to put me up for the night. We got involved in discussions about Marian, her family and our families. Maria, someone I knew 32 years prior, made a very interesting statement. She stated, "Do you want to know what I notice about you? I notice your head is up. You never seemed to have your head up when I used to know you. I noticed it at the funeral also, during that weekend, your head is up, you carry your head up."

Maria saw my head up. I asked her what it meant, not meaning a hockey term that you are supposed to play with your head up looking where you are going, or the expression for when someone is feeling down about themselves. She noticed my head was up, meaning I was aware, and vibrant. She continued, "This is what contributes to your entire aura, your look, and it is where the beauty comes from."

I was stunned, but after thinking about it, I agreed with her. My head was up because I felt amazing about myself. I had the confidence to do anything, and am grateful for everyone in my life. The other thing she shared is that in the end, I made it possible for Marian to have what she really wanted out of life. A family, and the chance to be a mother. That was her goal all along, that is what she really wanted to be. Despite her advanced degrees and writing ability, she wanted to be a mother, and we did everything we could to make that happen, and I should feel good about that.

Sitting there speechless with a lump in my throat, I felt good. The next day, after checking in on my father-in-law on the way back, of course with our On the Side subs, I reflected on how grateful I am on my five hour drive back home. Grateful to have friends that I can count on, both new and old, and that they can count on me. I realized how much love I could have is infinite, and I can show it and say it to anyone. I came to the conclusion that all that has happened in the last five years, and particularly in the last three years of therapy and the transition, that I love myself, and that is ok, and I am not afraid to say it.

37

IT HAS BEEN MY PRIVILEGE

I HAVE LEARNED A LOT THROUGH THIS LIFELONG experience. The timing of my therapy and my coming out process was engineered for me to be able and prepared both mentally and emotionally to care for Marian during her illness. Along the way, it was just a little less than a year before two major events happened: the Covid-19 Pandemic that shut down most of the world for months, substantially changing the way the world works, and the murder of a Black man named George Floyd by the police in Minnesota. Both of these disturbing events exacerbated an already split political landscape where the country was divided, causing a profound impact on a pivotal election that would certainly determine the direction of the country for years to come.

This was quite an interestingly-timed moment. Here I was, a newly released queen that had spent over fifty years of my life locked away in a vault. While in the vault, I used an alter-ego to travel through my life experiencing a parallel life, which was my life as a dude. I endlessly attempted to find my way out of the vault and live the life I was supposed to live, at the same time doing everything I could to hide and keep myself safely inside that vault.

Being out for a year before these events made for more than an interesting and well-timed moment for my development and my journey, even though the world was in turmoil. The initial spread of the Covid shutdown most of the world, at the same time when the many people of color and of underrepresented groups within our country felt violated and had had enough. Many folks had nothing to lose. Thousands of people took to the streets to protest this avoidable killing of a Black man, while everyone was instructed to stay at home and work inside, and only essential workers were allowed to work.

I was upset at the murder, and the more coverage of the event I watched I got angrier. The consternation with police was new to me and, although I realized that Black people were often discriminated against for jobs, housing, and almost everything in everyday life simply for existing, I knew there had to be more to this police thing, and this must not be an isolated situation. I also knew that I could not just go and ask my closest BIPOC friends for the intimate details on this–I had to do the work of seeking out learning opportunities. Though it's not the same, there are parallels with BIPOC people getting killed by police and trans people getting killed by homophobic and transphobic people. All of this killing of members of underrepresented groups came to feel the same to me, all of them unacceptable.

What could I do? How could I contribute? I could continue to read the news on the internet and watch the cable news channels, but this was really becoming much more personal to me, and I needed to learn from real people exactly what it is that they are angry about and the root causes so I may be able do something about it, and maybe relate it to my group of people. I found a local social action group, All Of Us, and found out about their rallies, protests, and educational opportunities. I wanted and felt I needed to attach to a group, offer my unconditional support, and to listen and learn exactly what Black people go through on a regular basis.

I had no idea prior to this point in time exactly why Black

people are so afraid of the cops, why some have a difficult time making a comfortable life for themselves, and other pertinent issues. Growing up as white, cis-presenting heterosexual man in a purplish metropolitan area (St. Louis) in a red state (Missouri), I did not see what Black people were complaining so much about. Why did they not just pick themselves up by their bootstraps and go about their lives? As time went along throughout my adulthood, I began to realize how Black people are discriminated against, and what many white people think about people of color unconsciously and otherwise. It really drove the point home after I came out and reflected on how I grew up with my grandma's and grandpa's using the n-work to speak about people of color as free and easy as they were breathing. The n-word was just another word in the vernacular of the time in the early 1970s and through the 1980s. What was not a part of the vernacular in my world at the time was the concept of privilege, and how much easier life was for those with white skin, a penis, and an attraction to women. I allegedly checked all of those boxes, and when I started to see affirmative action in employment and education situations, I got upset that myself and people like me would "lose" opportunities because of these accommodations. I realized what I actually knew deep inside, that I never lost anything to anyone based on anyone's gender or their skin color.

Throughout my life and my perspective from the vault, I considered very carefully what I would be throwing away if I would have been a girl, or if I did anything to become one, if that was at all possible. If I was a woman, I would have expectations to look a certain way or else the guys would make fun of me, or think significantly less of me, due to my numerous encounters with men, including friends, acquaintances, and strangers. The social system was such that the men's perspective was the default one, and the women had to adjust to it. And this is before I really understood appalling recent history when women could not vote, could not have their own bank account or have their own credit card without a husband's approval, which was rectified during my lifetime. MY LIFETIME, can you believe that ?!? Even though it was not defined as privilege, I understood the immense comfort I would be giving up in order to come out of the vault and be myself, to say nothing about the abuse waiting for me for dressing up like a girl in public as a person with a penis, which was horrifying to witness and read about, and even more terrifying to imagine happening to me. I was among friends and groups of guys on many occasions who would say horrible things about queer people that they know or see in public, and talk about how they wanted to do tremendous damage to that queer individual. These people were simply living their lives, trying to navigate not only the discriminatory policies and behavior against them, but also the hatred that would present itself at almost any time. Stories were told about queer people getting beat up, hospitalized, and killed. I've been to comedy clubs about three different times in my life, in the 1990s, and all three shows happened to make a man in a dress the punch line of several jokes. Late night talk shows featured this as well, along with the fake news tabloids such as the Star and the National Enquirer, which were very popular in those days. Many movies I saw, such as The Crying Game (1992) featured an affair between a man and a woman. After the woman reveals her penis, the man goes away to puke in the bathroom. Ace Ventura, Pet Detective (1994) and The Naked Gun 33 ½ (1994), also showed puking with the public outing of the trans-femme character, but also included long visual comedy scenes to ridicule this character after being attracted to the characters throughout the movie. I do not really remember the ending of The Crying Game, since I could only think about the reactions of the love interest. I remember seeing the other two shows and really enjoying the comedies and, in particular, the main characters throughout. These scenes at the end of the movies gave me a much different impression of the movie, actually ruined it, but since I spent the entire time laughing throughout the movie, I could not talk about my disappointment, disgust, and anger to the people who accompanied me to these shows. I had to hold all of it in and act like I loved it.

While the differences in privilege pertaining to gender were rather clear to me, what I did not realize and likely would not have to experience is the discrimination people of color are subjected to. My daughter, a Chinese-American cisgender woman, was part of the "perfect minority" which I implicitly knew but did not realize consciously until being educated by Christa. I realized it very clearly during that time when Trump was blaming all Chinese people for the Coronavirus, and the insecurity that Jade felt at the time. In another example, I overheard a Zoom class that my son Alex, a 17-year Latino at the time, was in class online on the first day of his senior year when a classmate said, "Alex, you are an ugly fuckin (n-word)" before the class had started.

Marian, Alex, and I were all stunned, and the teacher jumped in right away, but took no disciplinary action, and there was no apology. These examples struck me loud and clear, where my own children were being referred to in a discriminatory way. With all of the tangible examples of discrimination, implicit bias, and other insensitive remarks that are now starting to appear on my newly developed radar, I could not sit back and not say anything when this behavior happens.

As I say this about my real world, I love who I see in the mirror every morning, and I go to work every single day and enjoy what I feel is a trans woman's privilege. I realize that trans woman's privilege does not exist or is ever talked about, however, I feel that I have enjoyed an increased visibility, and with that, a voice that carried. I feel I am showered with respect all over our campus, by my department, our area of student affairs, senior college administration, faculty that I interact with, visitors to campus, and students from all areas of campus. I had also been invited to participate in several on-campus committees: The Safety in Education committee, where we discuss Title IX and gender-based misconduct issues, and the History and Symbols committee, where we discuss names and other various aspects of our campus that may be problematic by modern day standards. Some of these include the concrete idol that students have painted at least every third night that turned out to be a Chinese Lion that was gifted to the college, which is sacred to Chinese culture. Additionally, the names of buildings that were named after slave owners or other soiled backgrounds, and our nickname, The Dutchmen. Many of these items were changed, and I was invited onto these committees and I felt I had a legitimate voice on them, aided by the increased confidence I gained with living my true self. My voice and my visibility as a trans woman has provided me with the avenue to present my ideas, and I no longer felt inhibited in any way.

Although I have had people unintentionally misgender me or deadname me out of habit, I have had just a few difficult stories to tell from the entire time I have been out. Am I unique? I am still not sure, although I would love to think not. I am 100% convinced that the next person to come out as trans publicly on campus will have a relatively similar reception, and an even easier and less frightening process in which to be themselves. Four years after my coming out on campus, Residence Services began to designate a gender affirming dormitory floor with 24 beds for gender diverse individuals, and that there are other faculty, staff, and many more students that are out gender nonconforming individuals. I am well aware that the gender non-conforming students do not enjoy quite the same privilege as I feel from every person and every corner of our campus. Anecdotally, I am told that not all of the BIPOC students and staff at our Primarily White Institution (PWI) feel the same comfort and sense of belonging as I do either. I realize with my position as a visible and respected staff member, there is a certain amount of inherent power in play here, which is in itself privilege. It is my mission to utilize this privilege and my visibility as a member of an underprivileged community to model my happy and confident demeanor to help change these stereotypes and attitudes of those who believe in these obstructive stereotypes. As much or more than that, I want the other people who may be hiding in their own closets, or vaults, or hideouts, or wherever they hide their true selves, to see someone who is happy, confident, and thriving, and hope they can see themselves doing the same or better than I am.

Just as importantly, I will always use my voice to try to change those who do not believe that people from underrepresented groups belong in the same space and deserve the same opportunities as anyone else does. I realize it is hard to change minds, but I believe I can change some minds, which would be a huge plus. I believe there are people who want to learn, and I have tried to take the time to help them with this process. I believe that when people see a trans person thriving in an area where trans people traditionally do not exist, they can change their minds. A tall order to say the least but nothing will change if I keep my mouth shut, and not try and fight for it.

38

WHAT CAN WE DO? I'M GLAD YOU ASKED

WHAT CAN WE DO? THAT DEPENDS ON WHO IS ASKING. For the next person waiting to come out but who is hiding, frightened about treatment in the form of personal attacks and or legislation put forth by cowards or Christians who, in the name of their god, will discriminate and push for laws against our community and our human rights, generated from general hate. Other reasons to be terrified is possible loss from lack of acceptance of a spouse, family members, friends, jobs, overall social status, and standing in groups you happen to be in. That is a lot to take into consideration, as the previous chapters describe.

Going through this is difficult, and you know who you are. Please get therapy by a queer competent and hopefully a trans competent therapist. There are plenty of podcasts and competent people on social media to follow, and even contact. The websites are out there, whatever you do to act on, please plan your course, and get help from a therapist for ideas on how to do this. Safety is a concern, especially in certain work and family dynamics. Find the people you trust, and know who you can tell. You will be vulnerable and you will grow and thrive once you embrace this vulnerability.

What about if you are not the person going through this, but just want to help someone that may be coming out? Or to just be a welcoming person to anyone who is going through something? Well, the previous chapters detail some ideas for you, but one of the simplest things has to do with pronouns.

I was scared and held everything in, but as I was reading email, watching a Zoom, scrolling social media, or anything else I see on other platforms, I always felt a bit of comfort when I saw pronouns listed in the email signature, social media, or included in a Zoom name. I felt, and still feel, that if someone who includes pronouns with their name, especially those who are cis and no one questions their gender, the person understands and respects us, and would be a safe person to be around. I appreciate seeing this and it is the single easiest way for an ally to do without getting into an uncomfortable discussion with someone. This person cares enough about us that they are secure enough to expose themselves to people that could possibly judge them.

I believe that the more people that use pronouns, the more common pronouns become on people's personal email, Zooms and social media, more people will add their own and it will become commonplace. More and more registration and informational forms that we are constantly filling out are asking for pronouns. It is my hope that all of them do. I also hope we can eliminate prefixes (Ms., Mrs. Miss, Mr., Mx., etc). Sir and ma'am can't go away fast enough, either. The odds of misgendering someone decrease significantly by removing the use of sir or ma'am. It seems very patriarchal that women have Mrs., Miss, and Ms to identify them, to tell the world if they are married or not, but the men have only one prefix. Why is it important that society know the marital status of women and not men?

Even better, why do we need them in the first place? To be

polite? Our society is getting a lot more informal, and I have yet to talk to someone who has been misgendered and thinks of this address as polite. This does not only apply to gender non-conforming people, it applies to people who may just wear their hair long or short, of some men have very fine features or their gestures that may make them appear to be feminine to most people, and some women may wear their hair short and appearing to look like a man is expected to present themselves. Androgyny is common these days, and it is terrific to witness. In the 1980s, pop music stars such as Chrissie Hynde, Annie Lennox, Boy George, and Prince made their image with a look of the opposite sex assigned at birth. Add Twisted Sister, an all male band who wore women's makeup, and other glam rock bands in that era. Who can forget David Bowie, whose crossdressing and androgynous look was iconic a generation prior to the glam bands. While I was not into all of the music of these artists and others, I secretly worshiped their look. I had that pathway blocked in my head that any interest shown in anyone of a "gender bending" appearance could make me guilty by association, according to the rules and regulations of my vault.

I realize you are reading this book as a good person, and you are not an asshole, and truly want to help assist our community. You can be nice and supportive, and also go to do more research. A perfect example of this is Beth, our Associate Athletic Director and a significant role model for me, not only as a woman, but as a person, and an athletic administrative professional. When Jim, Beth, and Joanne approached Gretchel and asked how to do things and Gretchel invited them all to the presentation on LGBTQ+ for her DEI class, she contacted me about a speaker she heard, and thought I would love to meet this individual and hear one of their talks. I went, and learned alot from this individual. That small gesture meant so much and had a lasting impact on me.

Another small but significant event happened at our department fundraising golf outing that she oversees. The outing took place about a month before I sent the letter to everyone, I was there to help out where needed wearing a purple women's cut v-neck t-shirt, a pair of black capri pants with purple piping, purple converse sneakers and a small, purple elastic headband that I used to hold my hair back and give me what I thought was a more feminine look. I was taking another chance, this time in front of our entire department and other friends and boosters of the athletic department. I was not sure how people would react, which helped make the situation feel incredibly vulnerable, but I went for it. Beth, who I was working with during the time before when the golfers were checking in, made it appear that nothing was wrong at all, nothing to see here. After a bit, Beth approached me and in a hushed tone, "Your headband is falling off."

I immediately became nervous, but in control. Still in the vault but with ventilation inside lately, thinking if I did not fix it right away, someone might see it and tell everyone, or someone might take a picture of it, post it, and becomes viral, I would be ridiculed and be shunned by the coaches and fans, and EVERYONE I KNOW!

Under control, I went inside and simply fixed the headband, and made sure I placed it so this would not happen again. The entire time I was so grateful for Beth for mentioning it and making sure I kept my dignity. Those five seconds it took Beth to tell me may have come and gone to her, and she may have forgotten all about it, but it meant the world to me at that time. It gave me the confidence to be myself and I can move on, knowing beyond a shadow of a doubt that she has my back, and if I would lose everyone else, which I already know would not happen, I knew I would still have her as someone who believes in me. This was huge, and there are many other examples of her watching out for me, particularly pointing out (several times) that I have a tag on my garment, so often that it had become something we almost joke around about.

Not long after this, most of the golfers had checked in, practiced their putting, and told their jokes about how they would not be able to hit the ball. A man who appeared as though he was a few years older than I was at the time approached me by himself, away from his playing partners. He walked around the tables that were joined together to make a corner, looking at the raffle prizes, and bought a few tickets. He then came back around the tables to me, and said, "I really like this! I really like this outfit, the colors. It looks great."

Inside the vault for the next second I was thinking something like 'Wha wh wh what? A dude said what? Hmm, this is really nice. What the heck is happening right now??!? Jesus Christ!" but what I said was, "Thank you very much, I really love these colors; I have always loved purple."

"Well it looks great, I like purple too, and you look great." He may have said that, or something like "Purple looks great on you, I am proud of you." or "I love what you are doing and I am here to support you in any way," I don't really remember exactly, but I was stunned. It was probably something like the former quote but with a meaning of the latter quote. I know it was supportive and as validating as anything that had been said to me by a stranger to that point. I felt great, and those two events catapulted me to the next level of euphoria increased my confidence exponentially. Again, this gentleman did not need to do this, and he could not have any idea of how much that gesture catapulted my development.

As time moved on with the "business as usual" mantra, other little examples have shown up in small ways, some that I don't always realize right away. Knowing me for years and years as a guy, and working with facilities, it is common to have to enter restrooms and locker rooms, and often with other guys from facilities or with Jim and others when part of a renovation or an upgrade. Before, we would not enter the women's locker rooms without first having a woman enter before us to check if it is ok for males to enter. Lately, while working on women's locker room renovation, Jim asked me very naturally to enter to check to see if he could go in. As much as I am used to that now, I was not then and it still feels good when thinking about the natural ease of the request.

The word Belonging has recently been added to the Diversity, Equity and Inclusion moniker. Belonging is being welcomed by any person and all people in the group, and being comfortable within the relevant community. To belong is just as important as simply being included. To belong, at least to me, is to be a comfortable and functional member of the community, treated as any other member despite what underrepresented group they are in, how many people actually look like them or how long they have been a member of it. For me, this is a significant factor in my mental health and my overall outlook.

One small act that contributed to a large sense of belonging is when Beth included me in an email to all of the women in our department announcing a Women In Sport conference over Zoom open to any woman working in collegiate athletics. In November, 2020, I received this, and I immediately thought that I would love to go to this, and signed up on the spot. I was giddy about being in a group of women as an actual member of the women's gender.

A couple of minutes later I realized that I was on that email in the first place. It was no surprise that it was Beth that included me in this, but I was still really touched that happened. The two seconds that Beth took to throw my name on the email gave me such a sense that I actually have made it, I have accomplished the seemingly impossible task of being a woman among women. I have never taken that for granted, and still do not, although I had stopped walking around as if I do not belong in a women's restroom or women's spaces anymore, and I feel I am worthy of being called a woman. A small gesture like this had such a large impact on who I have become and the reason I feel the way I do.

The most natural thing to say to people who have a name and pronoun change is something along the lines of "I will try, this is going to be hard, I know I will make mistakes, if I do please don't be mad at me. I will try."

I totally understand why someone would say that. Read that again, or have someone read it to you about something you have changed in your life, or even how you would feel if it was said to you about my situation. How does that sound when said to you? I understand it is new to some, but I can't help but to hear that I am a burden for people. Please understand that it is easy for me and people like me to tell if it is a mistake out of habit. If it happens, just apologize and move on. You do not need to take all day and get sidetracked from the conversation apologizing, even though you are trying and feel bad about it. We appreciate that you realize the mistake. Making a big deal out of it makes it about you, and gives us more attention that we are different and difficult.

The bottom line is, and I am speaking generally here, but we all know when someone is saying your deadname on purpose to hurt us and saying the wrong honorific (sir, ma'am) to be a jerk. If they have beliefs that someone should not transition, that does not mean that the person should not use my name. We all know people that go by different names than they were given at birth, just as we all know many people shorten their names, and some of them change them back when they get older. Some people are called by their middle name their entire life, and some people go by their nickname, something that has no connection to their birth name at all. When people get married, often one of the people changes their last name. This is no different at all. Even if someone does not believe that this should happen because of something religious, our name should not matter in that. They are just being transphobic, or an asshole, or both. If you will not use our name because you don't want to and would rather be an asshole, you are an asshole.

Speaking of religion, please don't use the religious excuse that your religion says that it is not natural to change, or god does not make mistakes, or any of this nonsense. I am and other people like me are on this earth experiencing what we are experiencing and telling the world about it. The people with religious excuses use their own beliefs to denounce how I feel, how others feel, or how anyone else should live. If you believe in a god, then god made me this way, and I was able to discover a way to be myself, who I feel I am. Those that have faith that a god exists and for Christians need to follow Jesus Christ, who according to legend took care of the poor people, the sick people that society shunned and others that were not part of the wealthy, 'in' crowd. I am living my life KNOWING what I feel inside and who I am, and what makes me happy. If Jesus was as the believers say he was, he would clearly approve, and apparently did, since trans people have been around forever. In short, you do not get a religious excuse.

To get to the point, the most direct and to the point that I heard from a gender non-conforming speaker about this subject was, "Be a good person, don't put people down." In simpler terms, "Don't be an asshole."

For those who are already out and have transitioned into who you are, my advice is simple: Be yourself and be proud of who you are, and most of all, be safe.

As for me, after five plus years of hormones, I have been very busy working on various endeavors. Some have been mentioned, along with others such as writing this book. I have been busy with working on the Team Trans board of directors. It is exciting to be able to contribute to this amazing entity, and to learn from some very impressive individuals. Along with my involvement with Team Trans, I have met a significant person with whom I have become close with, and we have been partners for almost three years. Laur, my non-binary teammate, is an amazingly special person, very intelligent, organized, and personable. I am confident that no one cares about me more than they do, and came around at a time when I was not looking for anyone and did not expect to meet anyone. We are now engaged ever since they arranged a proposal at our 2023 Team Trans weekend, with over seventy people on the ice for practice, and made up a story about how we should be wearing microphones with a documentary crew in place to record our weekend. It was unbelievably touching and an amazing feeling. With this team and Laur living with us, I feel very strong, confident and happy each day.

EPILOGUE: CHALLENGE ACCEPTED

A number of years ago, when the kids were around four and five years old, Marian and I would take the kids to Freedom Park in Scotia, NY, just a five minute drive from our house. Directly next to that is Jumpin' Jacks, a seasonal burger and ice cream place with outdoor seating and a 1950s vibe. During the summer Saturday evenings, a different band would play on the outdoor covered stage right on the edge of the Mohawk River each week. We would treat all four of us to burgers, fries, and ice cream, and head over to the amphitheater directly next door to the iconic local summer attraction to listen to whatever band was playing that night.

To my surprise one night in August, there was a giant crowd with barely anywhere to sit. Alex Torres and His Latin Orchestra, a popular Salsa band, was playing. When I say they were playing, they had the packed crowd in a frenzy. I had never heard this type of music before and I immediately fell in love with the beat of the salsa music, and I was amazed at how so many of the dancers were on the dance floor area all knowing exactly what they were doing, changing dance partners after each song. I was dying to try it, and wanted so badly to somehow be part of it.

So a white, cisgender, heterosexual married man and father (at least that was the role I was playing in the game of life at the time) wanted to join this group of accomplished dancers, most of whom seemed to me to speak Spanish with one another. The palpable energy of this vibrant live music of which I did not understand a single lyric took me to another place that I had never been before. The beat, the energy and passion of the band and joy of all of the people that were dancing, along with the apparent camaraderie with one another left a permanent impression on me. One of the only times I felt like I was peeking out of the vault is when I asked Marian if she might be interested in learning how to dance like this.

"No."

That was it. That was the end of it. I laughed at the comedic moment, but I had never forgotten this night. I realized a few things in the few weeks and years since: I am in a vault, of which I cannot let myself out, meaning I could not make myself vulnerable to actually dance with and in front of people, and the kids were so young leaving no pathway to get away from them for times to learn to dance a dance that was foreign to me. I did realize, however, that ALL dance was foreign to me. I can't dance, I have never danced, and I did not see myself able to let myself out of the vault to learn this. I also did not know where the time away from work would come from in the fall, winter, and spring months. So I settled for going each summer when that band was playing there.

Fast forward to late June 2022, Laur being a Latinx person was able to be convinced to come with me while they were visiting town and we took a lesson. I remember it being so fun, with a lot of people there and Lenny, the teacher, being so nice to us. We would work on a move, then we would dance that with a partner, with all the couples positioned in a circle. I realized how awful I was and how awkward this felt, as if my feet were two concrete blocks. After we practiced with one of the people, the followers would rotate to another person to dance with.

I did not expect to be a pro after the first lesson. I knew I made many mistakes. As a woman, I became a follower, as I did not want to give off any vibes whatsoever that I would be a leader. I vowed to stay on course with my new gender role (typically the men lead and the women follow, but that is not a rule). The looks I received from some of the leaders were impossible to not notice, and some of them did whatever they could to stay as far away from me as possible while still dancing with me. On the other hand, many of them were very nice and treated me as they would any other girl in the place. Still others I could tell were making up their mind. I did not let that ruin my night. After the lesson, I was hooked. I could not wait to get back.

Laur went back home to Wisconsin, and I went to another lesson, and I loved it. I realized that not everyone would know "what" they were dancing with but many treated me with respect during the lesson.

Three days later there was a social dance. I could not wait to go. There was a lesson for the first hour, which I desperately needed, and then a social dance for the next three or four hours. I did not know what to expect, but I wanted to do the best I could and participate as much as possible, knowing I was not the least bit proficient at this.

After working individually with a few steps and moves, they broke us up into leads and follows, then asked the leads to find a follow. A man named John came across the room in my direction, accidently knocking into a person to get to me and ask me to be his partner. He had been in this community for many years and knew how to dance. I was unclear why a random dude I had never met had to find me with such a purpose, but I felt good about this. When we rotated, it was similar to the other night when some people would treat me with dignity while some of the others acted as if I had Covid and wanted nothing to do with me. I expected that. Once the social dance started, John came to me and asked to dance, helped me out with some of the moves and made me feel comfortable. The owner of the studio and instructor asked me to dance, as well, then the original guy again. I danced in three of the first six songs, which gave me some hope that this would be a fun night.

After that, I would ask many leads to dance, and not a single person would. Some said no, some waved me away, others made up stories about being too hot, needed water, sprained an ankle, needed a break, and had to go to the bathroom. All the while it was beginning to dawn on me that no one wanted to dance with me. I watched the entire group with interest to check out some of the apparent inexperienced leads that may stoop low enough to dance with me, and at the same time watching the apparent experienced followers to see how they were doing it. My eyes kept following a tall, lovely woman who was an amazing dancer, so good that I could not identify anything I was taught due to all of the extra moves that she added to everything she did. It took me at least an hour and a half to realize that I was watching in amazement this talented young lady who exudes more joy than anyone I had ever seen doing something they love. Once I realized this, I also concluded that I was not going to dance anymore, and that I likely was in the wrong place for me that I would never be proficient enough for this type of activity, one that I had never, ever attempted before due to my self-imposed ban from anything that could possibly be construed as feminine throughout my entire life. I also realized this was a lonely time that I really did not strike up a conversation with anyone, after my initial attempts. Since coming out, I was not one to keep to myself, here I was with my new extraverted nature somehow suppressed, and I was wondering if I may have tried the wrong new hobby.

As this conclusion was forming inside my brain and I was starting to get ready to go, the tall girl approached me with her hand out and asked me to dance. The emotions I felt at the time were many and in opposition. I was amazed that this young, talented dancer, who I determined to be far and away the best in this crowded room, while at the same time realized I had sat there for a little over two hours doing nothing and my muscles were stiff. Totally intimidated, I believe I said something like, " Are you sure, I just started, I'm not that good."

With a warm, friendly smile, she replied with something like, "That's ok, let's do it anyway."

I remember being nervous just walking out there, and I tried as hard as I could to at least dance well enough to not waste the time of the best dancer in the room. It turned out that she was most helpful, and showed me how to do some of the steps. It only took the first twenty seconds of the dance and her first smile and word of encouragement to feel relaxed, comfortable, and not afraid to make mistakes, which was a good thing since I made many of them. After I thanked her and got her name, Isabel, I could feel myself floating. I could not wait for the next dance, and the next night that I could come to dance, and I remember not caring if anyone danced with me the rest of the night. On my way out of the building, I struck up a conversation with the original guy that asked me to dance. He asked me if I had fun, and I told him of my experience. He shared with me that one of his best friends was trans and that he wanted to see that I was somehow taken care of. We had one more dance before I left for home.

The joy of the few dances I had that night made an immediate impact on this novice dancer, and I knew while driving home afterward that night that I would put in the work to become at least a competent dancer as long as I enjoyed myself while doing it. I was beyond excited that someone paid attention to a trans woman in a large crowd where trans people seem to not be. The major highlight of the night was that Isabel, the best and most dynamic dancer in the room, approached perhaps the worst dancer in the room who did not dance the majority of the night without a single bit of judgement. The guy who danced with me did it *because* I was trans, which I appreciated. Of all of the leads in the packed room, only one made it over to include this beginner who at the time was really needing to feel included. Over the last three years I have come to really admire Isabel, adore her actually, and am honored to have her as a friend, an instructor, and an idol. I never let her forget the impact that gesture had on me as I often refer to her as "My Favorite Lead." It is 100% true.

Learning these dances was a slow process for me, as it was so far from what I had trained to do decades ago as a hockey goalie. I loved learning it, and really took it to heart when people would take extra time to give me feedback to make me better. While there were (and still are) men that would stay away from me at the social dances, I was getting to know more and more of the women. I was able to approach the women and start a conversation, and they were able to do the same for me. Before I knew it, I had dozens of friends, all of whom I could talk with and know something about whenever I saw them out. A number of the more accomplished dancers actually took me over to the mirror to practice or work on something I am not proficient in or things that do not come naturally to me. After six or so months of invading this community just learning a new skill, I was beginning to feel as if I was welcome. While this feeling accelerated through the next couple of months, I was beginning to make more connections with the men who were leads. The more leads that would dance with me, the more I got to dance, and the better I became. I figured there was a chance they would dance with me as long as I was competent at it, or at least would establish a relationship with them then they may dance with me. I did that more and more often and was able to dance a bit more, all the while learning more from many. I would ask them to dance, do the best I could and let my joy shine through.

There was a night I turned the corner. There is a very popular dancer, a very big man named Derrick. This man was tall, had a large personality, and danced with endless energy, requiring multiple t-shirt changes throughout the night, and he appeared to dance with everyone in the room with a huge smile on his face. I was there with Laur and I told them that this was the night I would do this, I would dance with Derrick. I was feeling more confident about my skills, and I felt I would be on the way to making it if I danced with Derrick. I just wanted to experience the joy that all of the other followers were having while dancing with this guy. Toward the end of the night, long after Laur wanted to leave, I reached the moment. Derrick was on the far side of the room in what I refer to as the Executive Lounge (strictly my word for it), a little alcove just off of the dance floor with a couch and a loveseat, and that was where a lot of the very accomplished dancers would hang out. Derrick was sitting by himself, a rare moment, possibly contemplating leaving. I made my move, darting across and half kiddingly asked Derrick, "Would you like to dance, because I would really like to see what it is like to dance with the best dancer in the room."

With his head facing downward and the largest grin developing on his face, he stood up and held his hand out. I was amazed! This guy was the same guy I saw dancing with everyone else as if each particular dance was the most important dance of his night. It was so fun, and he was very kind, telling me that I was a good follower. I realized he was being kind, since I was not a good follower, but I was an improved follower than I was the third night in the studio dancing with Isabel. I was excited that I had the guts to even speak to this large, iconic figure that I soon got to know as one of the most genuinely nice, friendly and humble people that I have ever met. He has asked me to dance every social dance ever since.

As I am meeting these people, I have felt more and more at home in and around the community. The more I went to the various lessons, I have been impressed at the level of instruction, and with that and what I am able to learn from the social dances by watching and doing, I felt myself improving. One day I received a message from one of the outstanding female dancers in the area that she was starting a dance performance team, and that she had the choreography for a Bachata song that any of the women that could commit to the practice sessions could join. I was elated to be sure. I realized that skill was not why I received an invitation, but all the women in the area did, and one of those women was *me*. I was four years into my transition and I have yet to take this for granted. I went for the first few weeks, and it was very difficult learning the moves, putting them together, being sexy doing it, and keeping up with the other girls who were all accomplished dancers. I began falling behind and realized that I was out of my league, especially since I did not have the time to practice on my own at that time of the year. It was a great learning experience, but the large reward that came out if it was that my name was included with all of the *women* in the community. I was considered one of the women. And I was included in the community. This feeling of inclusion never gets old. Five and a half years after I came out and have been living as my true self, I still do not take it for granted that women would include me within their group, let alone treat me as if I just belong there, not just that they are doing me a favor by including a trans girl that will not go away. This is the feeling I had long hoped would develop, that I would walk into a room with whatever community I was in, be it hockey, the campus, the local area, or the dance community. In hockey, I am treated as Brianne, a coach and an administrator. In the dance community, I am a woman and follower that likes to dress in loud, colorful outfits with many friends in the building each time I arrive.

I was able to become part of a smaller group within the community when Felix, one of the instructors in the area, started teaching Salsa Rueda, which is a very fun and energetic form of dance where the dancers are paired up with a lead and follow, positioned in a circle formation. There is one caller, and the whole group does the move that the caller yells out, many moves requiring switching partners and continuing the dance. It was a lot to learn, especially the names of the moves being in Spanish, but so much fun. Felix brought an energetic vibe to the classes and really made things fun. The group had a few chances to perform in front of people at the social dances, which was the first time I ever performed in front of people. To do this was exhilarating, and such a great format with the read/hear and react with changing partners and working together as a team. We knew the moves but not necessarily what the caller would call. Rueda became my favorite form of dance that I have experienced.

After taking classes for quite a while with Isabel and her partner David, they had decided to put together a Salsa dance performance team. This would be my first experience with choreography. Even though I was an unofficial accomplished actor playing an athletic male character for over 50 years, that acting experience was not scripted; it was a reality show. Anything that had to do with scripts made me incredibly self conscious and very unconfident. However, I was intrigued by this as a way to break through this fear and apprehension, and since I loved and trusted the instructors, I was all in. We started in late January 2024 with learning the choreography, and with team members adding on and dropping out, it took a while to sort itself out. This meant the performance date continued to be delayed, providing a longer time to prepare. This preparation included learning the choreography, learning how to execute each move, where each move fit into the routine, the various positions on the floor, and the many different options of interaction with my partner. This process was beyond overwhelming and far out of my comfort zone, but as time went by, I became more comfortable with the song and the moves, learning a lot about performing and dance concepts along the way. Then comes our first performance in mid July.

The day of the performance I was over the top excited, while being a bit nervous and relatively confident that I could finish all of the moves while keeping up with the beat of the fast music. I was so excited to realize that the rehearsals, the extra time I put in to learn the routine, the bonus time David and Isabel worked with me by myself in their apartment, the countless times listening to the music, and going through in my mind what move came next and what I needed to do to make that move better. I felt pretty well at our last rehearsal the night before, but this was game day and I had to be ready.

All of these thoughts going on within the overarching emotional realization over this entire experience: I am putting myself in the most vulnerable situation that I have been in since my early months of busting out of the comfort and safety of the vault. Ever since high school, I worked to perfect my hockey skills, then my coaching and recruiting skills, and my ice maintenance skills, for 44 years, I had been doing what I was good at, and now I was putting myself out there doing something completely new, and something of which I had no expertise and in a position I never would have had I remained in the security of my own vault. My reply to myself was a hearty, "Bring It On, Bitch, I Got This!"

If it was only that easy. Our group showed up at 6:00 pm to practice for a 11:00 pm performance. Walking into the building felt like game day on the night of my first college hockey game. In a pink skirt and a darker hot pink sleeveless top with my Team Trans Unicorn logo on it I walked in with my red dress on a hanger and a bag full of items I would need for the night: a makeup bag, a dress to wear at the social dance prior to the show, my white hair ribbon that goes with the red and white team colors, two pairs of dance shoes, an apple, a banana, a protein bar, two cans of Downeast cider, along with my purse. I found a place in the auxiliary dance room adjacent to the main room where our group would stage ourselves. An elevated, smaller dance floor was there, taking up around two-thirds of the room. The one side of the floor went all the way to the wall, with strings of white lights illuminated on it. I had butterflies in my stomach. Good butterflies. Nervous butterflies. I always looked at butterflies as a good thing, since the event I was taking part in means so much to me. I had eaten so long ago, but exactly like my hockey days, I wasn't hungry. I was good with drinking water. I also knew I could not sit still, so I walked around and practiced some of the moves in the mirror.

Around 6:15 pm we spent time on the floor in a tech rehersal walking through our positions so we had a good idea of where to go and what it looked like to be in all of these positions as we maneuver around the floor.

At 10:05 pm, we started to get into our performance outfits, and began to focus a bit with some of the moves. I went into a closet in the back of the auxiliary room to change into my red dress. The entire room was a bit stuffy so I kept moving around and drinking water, and not allowing myself to fall into a lethargic feeling that could play with my nerves. I still had my dance sneakers on, waiting until it was almost time to run through the routine. At that point, I took the makeup bag, and Isabel and Melissa had the same idea. The three of us walked together through the crowded dance floor near the stage to the women's bathroom, where we all began to lean over the counter to see ourselves closely in the mirror as we got our faces ready. While the occasional girl would squeeze between us to wash their hands and say something in support of us. I felt a camaraderie I had not felt before as we were all chatting about putting on makeup and doing our hair while we were just doing just that. I stopped for a second and I realized that moment was such an important one I rarely experience. A feeling of warmth went through me as I realized that these two amazing women who had so much more experience at dancing than I did and had so, so many more years of being a woman than I had, were naturally treating me as their equal. I belonged there in that moment, doing a women's thing while getting ready to do a dance thing. I remember vividly feeling normal. Normal in a way of preparing for an important event with a group, and the attention to detail, the positive thinking, and making sure everything is just right. Normal also in a way that I was with two other women in a women's restroom putting on makeup and fixing hair and outfits even though this was not something I was particularly used to. I could not even fathom the amount of gratitude I had for everyone that had helped me and most of all encouraged me up to that point.

Walking back to our room, I had all the confidence I needed to go out there and fit in with the group. Once we all arrived back in the seldom used, somewhat musty room, the music was audible, yet muted. The lighting in that room was unevenly dispersed, with the lines of white lights the most bright. I sat down and put on my black dance shoes with only a one inch heel. I had a difficult time latching the strap on my left shoe, getting more frustrated and anxious as the time went along. Feeling myself spending more brain energy getting upset that I could not latch a strap on my relatively new shoes. I did not want the negative thoughts in my head and nervously asked Melissa to attach it for me as she was walking by. Once they were on and I was walking around practicing a couple of moves, I realized the straps on my shoes around the ankle felt loose. I never liked that unsupported feeling. I did not want the idea of tipping over due to my ankle not being supported so much that I had to compensate in any way to creep into my head at any point between now and after the performance. As the time was growing closer to the group practicing the routine I actually took both shoes off and tightened each ankle strap. I then was able to put them both on myself, relatively quickly, and I felt in control. I used to do the same routine with my skates before games, to be able to be in control of every move my feet make. These activities in both of my very happy places, playing goalie and dancing, I needed to have my feet secure so I can be as precise as possible for every move I make. I need this for confidence. I need this to keep me from thinking about my feet wobbling around inside the shoe and over compensating for each step that I would take, or worse, falling out of the move. I never wanted to be the one to let my team down, especially over something that I could control. I still don't. The same feelings, fifty years apart.

After group pictures and a couple of practice runs, David called us all together in a circle and told us how proud of us he was, and he knew we would do great out there. Everyone makes mistakes, but if it happens just laugh it off and keep going, the crowd likely will not know the difference. I was back to feeling confident, knowing that we would go out and crush it. Others chipped in with words of encouragement, and Kenoye gave us all a tip about what to look at while we are looking at the crowd, which helped a lot.

We then lined up to walk out, like we did so many times before, only this time we were waiting for the music to stop and the announcer to introduce us. The quiet was a bit unnerving, yet exciting. He seemed to keep talking and talking, and I felt my hands getting a bit sweaty. I looked around at the group, and forward again, with Isabel waiting ever so patiently at the front of the line with her partner, making me relax. I am not used to show business, and this is just the way it goes.

When we heard the announcer yell "Girasol" I looked outside the door where the crowd was loud and were right up to the line that we were to dance to. I saw many familiar faces, which made me feel calm. We heard our walkout music, and Isabel and her partner walked out to their positions to loud yelling and applause. Kenoye and I were next and once we heard our cue we followed them. I was doing my best to mimic Isabel, trying to add as much sass to my walk as I could. Once Kenoye dropped me off at my starting position, I felt nothing but self satisfaction and confidence. I knew I had this. Once in our starting poses, I was looking forward to the stage and instead of looking at the speaker stand, I made eye contact with Frankie, the DJ, and he gave an encouraging grin and head nod. I knew this was beyond thinking about it at this point--just go and let the music, the muscle memory, and the habits take over. Adding to the comfort was that with the other follows being so good that all eyes would (and should) be on them. Plus, my partner, Kenoye, was such an amazing lead that I knew I was far from a once scary place and in a calm and safe place. I remember thinking just before the music started, "This is so goddamn exciting! I can't believe it! This is so much fun!" If this is the only chance I would have at this, I was damn sure going to enjoy it, and enjoy being myself in front of everyone.

The song seemed to go so quickly, before I knew it we were walking back into the room before we returned to take a bow out in front of the crowd. The cheers, noise, and smiles brought such an exhilarating feeling. Then Camille, another dear friend, a great dancer and former team member, walked down the line handing us all a girasol—a big yellow flower—to represent the name of our group.

We then walked back to the room where everyone proceeded to hug. We could not wait to see it on video and work on the program and improve for the next time. I felt so much satisfaction and I couldn't stand still. I just wanted to hug everyone. Laur came in with an enormous smile on their face and gave me a huge hug, opened one of my ciders, and forced it into my hand.

We went out there and had a great performance as a group. I had a feeling I had never felt before. I realize I am not as talented as Melissa, my dear friend and confidant who I had become very close with through this entire process and the one who convinced me to include this experience in this book, or Isabel, my idol and the inspiration for me to pursue all opportunities within the dance. I did not believe it was possible that I would be in the same group on the same stage as these two beautiful people and dancers, but I WAS in the same group on the same stage as these two beautiful people and dancers. I respect these two ladies a great deal, and while I never had a doubt that I belonged with them in any group at any time, the moment of truth on stage was another story. Of course I had work to do to improve, but that didn't matter at that moment. The euphoric feeling that I had for more than a week after that night I came to realize was that I was provided the opportunity to earn the right to belong with them on a team of their level. No judgment, no hierarchy, just a feeling of pure joy to be treated as just one of the performers, one of the girls. And I accomplished just that.

I think of this feeling of inclusion and belonging every time I think of the laws that right wing politicians are trying to legislate against the rights of trans people when it comes to inclusion in sports, educational opportunities, access to health care, access to bathrooms that match our gender identity, and many others. All trans people should experience what I did on stage. I will never forget the feeling of the community's support of this, treating me with respect as a performer who worked hard to accomplish something that not everyone had the chance or the desire to do.

I have a lot of work to do with this and am proud of how far I have come as a dancer, and along with that how far I have come as a person, a partner, a parent, a friend, and a visible and vocal representative of the trans community. Above all that, I am happy and free. I didn't feel different, I felt normal, like myself.

My thoughts and dreams from under the bed fifty years ago came true, I am who I am supposed to be. Because of it, I have become the happiest person you know.

ACKNOWLEDGMENTS

After I transitioned, settled in on campus, and immersed myself into the LGBTQ community on campus and off, I walked into the Unity Lounge early for a presentation and our Director of Intercultural Affairs, **Dr. Gretchel Hathaway**, told me, "Brianne, you have a great story and it is very unique. You need to write a book." It had been something I always dreamed about but never thought I had the writing skills for. After sharing this feeling she said, "You have to get your story out there, it is important, and can inspire so many people. You can do it, just start writing ideas, and worry about putting it together later on." It took me a hot fifteen seconds to agree with her and decide to further lean into my vulnerability and tell my story in a way that was not in my skill set. I started writing ideas down that evening.

This decision took place during my wife **Marian Brinker's** illness, but that did not stop her from lending me plenty of writing tips that she used to impart to her students as a middle school writing teacher. Writing was her passion, not mine. Her advice and ability to proofread a couple of chapters was invaluable. As her illness intensified, her patience for me not being able to hear her the first time she tried to speak to me waned in a huge way, she asked that I stop my writing and put all of my attention on her. It was the right thing to do at the time.

I resumed this project close to a year later, and my new friend, partner, and currently fiance **Laur Rivera** would work together, and they would proofread my work. Their second set of eyes helped so much in the early on, going from a bunch of ideas to piecing things together. Their encouragement throughout the remainder of the process was invaluable. I am glad they could learn so much about my life from these initial ideas I wrote. Laur's contributions to the marketing effort were and continue to be invaluable.

I was beyond fortunate to have the amazing editor **Kate Turner**. She was very encouraging and managed to give me an immense amount of confidence by pretty much asking me to clarify and expand my ideas throughout the book. For a novice writer, I could not have been in better hands to learn what would and what likely wouldn't resonate with the reader. It was an invigorating learning experience to make her suggested changes.

I had been impressed the first day **Dr. Christa Grant**, interviewed for the Director of Intercultural Affairs at Union College. This thoughtful and dynamic individual became my role model and mentor in all things Diversity, Equity, Inclusion, and Belonging, and her advocacy thereof. She provided me not only the confidence to advocate and lead, but gave me a platform for my voice that was dying to escape from deep inside myself. Her own dedication to development in academia and as a person was inspiring .

I wrote, researched, edited, and queried a lot of this work in the company of my closest friend I've ever had, **Dr. Mercedes Victoria Mayna-Medrano**. Meche is very brilliant and driven to excel in every task she has with a tireless work ethic. Her discipline and dedication is infectious and inspired me to focus on this project that was far out of my comfort zone.

My dear dance friend, **Melissa Beall**, encouraged me, check that, strongly suggested/made me realize, that I need to include the most important activity that brought me life-changing joy for the last three years. She couldn't have been more accurate, thus is solely responsible for my dance story with the epilogue.